help,
i'm
dealing
with
trauma

It is true, we all have at some point in our lives experienced some form of what is called trauma. This book helps us to not only be honest with ourselves, but also be encouraged that there is hope for our traumatic life experiences. Reading this book will give you an assurance that "God is able" to lead you through the dark places, the painful places, the hopeless places, and yes, the angry places of your past—to bring you to a bright place of joy, peace, love, and hope. You will come to know that there is no limit to what God can do!

Rev. Eric C. Carson, Senior Pastor of First Baptist Church,
Chillicothe, Ohio

Lemuel Blackett shares with courage and truth his real-life story of personal trauma from growing up in a wounded family to the painful experiences in the marketplace and church. This book will encourage you to find good in the negative, faith in the midst of personal turbulence, and light when your life is dark. Lemuel reminds us that the human spirit is resilient and capable of healing from trauma's often-visible and hidden mal-effects with help, faith, and love.

Pablo R. Diaz, pastor and former Vice President
of Ministries of Guideposts

Honest, raw, transparent, and powerful are just a few words to describe Lemuel Blackett's *Help, I'm Dealing with Trauma*. His journey as recorded here is a must read for those dealing with relational trauma or the effects of childhood trauma. The insight it provides is invaluable for counselors and advocates as well. It offers truth, hope, and inspiration. By following Lemuel's journey, we see there is promise after pain if we don't give up. I highly recommend this book.

Kevin C. Hardy, Pastor of St. Matthews Unison Free Will Baptist Church,
New Haven, Connecticut

Tolstoy once stated that everyone thinks of changing the world, but no one thinks of changing himself. In this masterful work on taming his trauma, Lemuel Blackett leads the reader to the point of introspection. You'll leave this work wanting to change what's within so that you can change what's around!

Stephen Thurston, Executive Pastor of Salem Baptist Church, Chicago

In *Help, I'm Dealing with Trauma* Lemuel Blackett masterfully gives context to a common cry. He has written a must-read work for anyone struggling with trauma and its subsequent trials. From funerals to faith, Reverend Blackett invites the reader to join him on an intimate journey of self-discovery complete with a roller coaster of emotions and real-life experiences. So, strap in, hold on, and enjoy the ride!

Tisha Dixon-Williams, Pastor of First Baptist Church
of Bridgehampton, New York

help,
i'm
dealing
with
trauma

Real Talk, Real Encouragement,
and Real Healing

LEMUEL R. T. BLACKETT

lakedrivebooks.com

Lake Drive Books
6757 Cascade Road SE, 162
Grand Rapids, MI 49546

info@lakedrivebooks.com
lakedrivebooks.com
@lakedrivebooks

Publishing books that help you heal, grow, and discover.

Paperback ISBN: 978-1-957687-10-0
eBook ISBN: 978-1-957687-11-7

Library of Congress Control Number: 2022945209

This book often relies on the use of storytelling. It reflects the author's present recollections and information gathering of experiences over time. Most of the names of individuals or institutions and their characteristics have been changed, some events have been compressed, and some dialogue has been recreated. Please also be aware that some of the language used can be coarse but is there in context and to recount actual events.

Scripture quotations marked ESV are taken from the ESV® Bible (The Holy Bible, English Standard Version®). Copyright © 2001 by Crossway, a publishing ministry of Good News Publishers. Used by permission. All rights reserved.

Cover design: Mike Williams
Cover photo: Unsplash.com

I dedicate this book to my sisters Rae Samantha Bishop and Deborah Patricia Whall. And my little brother Karl Whall. I love and miss you every day. Rest in Peace!

CONTENTS

Foreword

It is said that some people come into your life for a season, while others come into your life to stay. As such I have been truly blessed to have obtained a God-ordained authentic relationship with my brother beloved in the person of the Reverend Lemuel Blackett. For a decade or so, we have assisted each other, shared mountaintop moments, and cried through valleys below as we have navigated through higher heights and deeper depths in our personal and ministerial existence. Treading through storms and triumphs, we have gained a better understanding of accountability as we buoy each other up trying to remain as steadfast and unmovable in an ever-evolving world.

In accepting all his own naked truths, through raw and transparent literary composition, *Help, I'm Dealing with Trauma: Real Talk, Real Encouragement, and Real Healing,* Lemuel has taken a pause from his own life experiences up until this juncture, a childhood included, to articulate boldly and brashly through pen on paper a raw and transparent literary arrangement that a multitude of us struggling to just exist can relate to. He has taken the results of disdain, disappointment, discouragement, and defeat from witnessing domestic violence as a youngster, experiencing death of close family members, unemployment in the secular work force, loss of friends, an aversion of acceptance of mental health support, and rejections in the ministry of the Gospel of Our Lord and Savior, Jesus, who became the Christ, and has produced a written symmetry that cries out, "Help, I'm dealing with trauma!"

With the shifting of the paradigms in the economy, government, the world, ministry, and church as we knew it, Lemuel's calling and being chosen to minster against a plethora of adversities—and the very essence of trauma, not just as a word, but as a genuine and unquestionable reality—gives the reader very simply, an "I have been there, done that" approach, and they need not feel that they are an island unto themselves. Thus, trauma is undeniable, but one should bolster enough emotional control to face it head on when it occurs. And what we experience as trauma should not only be life lessons for us, but also examples, platforms by which we aid someone else on a traumatic journey. It is said in the Kingdom of God that unless you have been through something and reached the other side you cannot witness to another. Through "letting it all hang out," Lemuel has grasped his own theology, his own "God talk" and opened the floodgates of not only his traumatic experiences but also his own modus operandi of healing as he humbly and compassionately pours out painful yet therapeutic nuggets of wisdom to anyone and everyone as they delve into this writing.

In conclusion, I rejoice and have a newfound respect of my brother beloved as he has "let go and let God," having obtained the courage to amass the ability to tell this story. I have been blessed to accompany him through some of these personal accounts and it is my prayer that as others partake in this reading, they receive the undeniable, profound, and deep riches of his testimony as he has become an overcomer by his written voice. This will encourage them to come out of the darkness and into the marvelous light!

Reverend Dr. Dawn Cherri Snell, MDiv, DMin

Introduction

trau·ma /ˈtroumə,ˈtrômə/ A deeply distressing or disturbing experience

I believe every human being has experienced trauma in some way. Traumatic experiences can distort your perspective. They can shape how you see the world, how you engage in politics, what religion you practice, the person you marry, and even the career path you choose. For instance, some people who have witnessed or experienced serious harm have chosen to become prosecutors or go into law enforcement. Others who have prematurely lost a loved one to a medical condition are inclined to become healthcare professionals.

Given the reality that trauma can influence the decisions we make in our lives, the way we respond to and manage trauma is incredibly important. This can determine whether we gain insight and grow stronger in the wake of a traumatic event or become mentally inhibited.

Unexpected tragedy can bring its own level of trauma. When you have planned how you will spend your day, week, month, or year and it is suddenly interrupted, it can be

1

traumatizing. For example, death, divorce, and layoffs can cause trauma. Sickness, the end of a friendship, or the dissolution of a business bring a level of trauma that is not easily manageable. Hoping that a new year brings new opportunities, only to be met with utter disappointment, is nauseating, to say the least. For example, many expected 2020 to be a year of possibility, of open doors, maximizing potential, travel, going back to school; the year of starting your own business, of trying something new, of turning dreams into reality.

For me, 2020 started off well. I ended 2019 with an extensive travel schedule and was excited to see what 2020 would bring. My wife, Kimberlee, was also preparing to pursue some of her own dreams in the new year. She had just begun her first semester for her second undergraduate degree in information technology and was laying the foundation to start a nonprofit that supported single mothers in minority communities. As for me, I had a full schedule of speaking engagements; my second book, *I Will Be Effective*, began gaining significant traction among churches; and I was offered a position as interim pastor at a historic church in Hartford, Connecticut. The first two months of the year were exciting, and I was making strides in my professional career. My friends and colleagues were also on the verge of major opportunities.

Then COVID-19 took over the world like a hurricane. What the novel coronavirus did to the world was deeply traumatic: school closures, job layoffs, devastated economies, home foreclosures, car repossessions, increases in child abuse and domestic violence, business closures, financial uncertainty, and food insecurities. And on top of that, we've experienced millions of COVID-related deaths worldwide, an ongoing assault on the Black community at the hands of trigger-happy, racist police officers, and a vitriolic and divisive presidential administration under former President Donald J. Trump.

This uncertain and new reality has caused the hopeful to lose hope and the faithful to abandon their faith. Such pervasive and widespread trauma has fueled distrust of the government, social media, and traditional media outlets. Trauma has set the stage for mental breakdowns, a lack of buoyancy, and fear of the future. The traumatic events many of us have endured have taken root in and contaminated our hearts and minds.

In my own life I've had to deal with my own traumatic situations. I was born in London, England. I am one of four children. My mother was from Guyana and my father was from Barbados. That West Indian upbringing was very toxic and traumatic. I grew up around violence, betrayal, heartbreak, sexual promiscuity, deceit, and gaslighting. There was never a dull moment in my household or extended family. My parents never shared their feelings verbally, and if anyone else did, they considered that a sign of weakness. As I got to learn more about my family, I learned that their behavior was passed down from one generation to the next. Fortunately for me I was able to escape some of that dysfunction. However, many of my cousins and all my siblings continued in that same pernicious behavior. To be completely honest, some of those family traits have carried over into my adulthood. So, when I recognize some of that familiar behavior from my childhood creeping in, I make it my priority to tackle it instantaneously before it festers into an uncontrollable series of events. As a husband and father of three amazing children, I've done my very best to prevent what

I've seen in my parents from affecting how I raise my children and interact with my wife. I've made it a personal mantra to refuse to mirror what I experienced growing up.

When I entered the ministry, I was warned it would be difficult and sometimes challenging, but I could have never imagined the number of scars I have from just trying to preach and lead God's people. The places that I thought would be safe spaces turned out to be hellholes. The sleepless nights and panic attacks were consistent in my everyday life. Every day was a new battle; every day seemed to get worse and worse until I made up my mind that this couldn't be what life is all about.

The good news is that I've discovered you can will yourself out of almost anything. Whenever I wanted something better, I spoke it, all day every day, until it came into existence. Does that work for everything? No. Will it work for most things you are trying to accomplish? Yes. Having a determined mindset can truly shift you from the negative to the positive. Optimism is my medicine; I take a dose daily. And what that does is reassure me that whatever I may be challenged with now will not always have a hold on me later.

For over a year now, to find purpose and wisdom in agony, I have used the time and space created by the pandemic to take inventory of my life. This has involved beginning to confront issues that have left deep emotional scars on my life. While I have caused harm and conflict that I must take responsibility for, others in my life have also harmed me. People in leadership positions in my life have failed to lead with integrity. Consequently, my vulnerability has been taken advantage of, my kindness considered weakness, and my honesty deemed confrontational. I have also had moments where I recognized if I did not seek assistance for my trauma, the trauma would have devoured me. Self-destruction would have been inevitable, and vengeance surely would have been my drug of choice.

My family is important to me. I am blessed with a wonderful, caring, loving, and supportive wife. I have three beautiful children who keep me laughing and energized. I am truly blessed. What scares me, though, is that I may project my trauma on to my loved ones. As I have strived to be the best husband and father I can be, suppressing my trauma has become part of my daily life. While stifling certain feelings has allowed me to maintain a healthy and loving environment for my family, it has also been physically and emotionally exhausting and damaging.

I finally sought out a therapist in February 2020. This was not an easy decision. I had arguments with my wife about it. In the past, I had judged others who went to counseling. I thought, *Black people don't go to therapy, we have Jesus*. That was, until December 2019, when I attended a men's conference as a speaker and a therapist was also in attendance to speak to the men. I admittedly tuned out the beginning of his talk until he described being of Caribbean descent. He also said he only works with Black men. My resistance to therapy lessened slightly. After about two to three months of staring at the therapist's card on my nightstand, I decided to reach out to him.

He connected with me on a level that no one else has ever been able to. He understood my background. The way he described how Black men in particular deal with stress and anxiety and the unhealthy coping methods Black men tend to be drawn to really captured my attention. I sat there thinking, *This man has somehow gathered inside information about my life*. That moment I made a decision that I needed to be his patient. It has been one of the best decisions I could have ever made.

Therapy has created a safe space for me to be vulnerable, transparent, and fully myself. I am so grateful that my wife encouraged me and that God allowed me to speak at that conference so that I could finally get the help I so desperately needed. Since seeing my therapist for over a year now, my marriage is stronger and my relationship with my children has been phenomenal. My life has taken a significant shift for the better, all because I have been able to do the continued work of dealing with my trauma of my family life, the losses I've experienced, and the difficult situations I've been in. I am so thankful for my relationship with God, and I am thankful that God put a wonderful therapist in my life.

I know it may be hard at first and you may have your reservations, but if you are serious about dealing with your trauma I would highly recommend seeking out a therapist who understands your culture. Make sure they can relate to what you are dealing with. The right therapist can help you change your life for the better. Alternatively, if you allow your trauma to go unaddressed and end up acting out of that unaddressed trauma, both you and your family will have to suffer the consequences.

Trauma can either be your launching pad or your detonator. My goal in this book is to share my journey in hopes it might support others in turning their own trauma into a launching pad to catapult them into their best life. Trauma is real. We can overcome it, but we must ask for help. Doing so is not a sign of weakness; in fact, it demonstrates courage to seek freedom from unbearable torment. You are not in this by yourself. You do not have to go it alone. This book is meant to help you lower your walls and finally declare, "Help! I'm dealing with trauma!" In this journey called life we are faced with a multiplicity of traumatic events. I have had my own fair share of traumatic situations that caused me to have a distorted perspective on life. My church experiences have been unhealthy; my upbringing has been complicated, violent, and confusing. My relationships with friends and lovers were quite toxic. During those times I wanted and needed something that would say to me, *Lem, everything is going to be okay and life will eventually turn around*. I want you to know that though you go through trauma, life will ultimately get better and your trauma in due course will subside. Hang in there; remain optimistic, because you are better than all that you have been through.

1
The Trauma of the Past
You Cannot
Change the Past

I have a bad habit of revisiting what happened years ago and replaying it with an up-to-date director's-cut version. Have you ever thought, *If I could go back in time, this is the way I would have handled that situation* or *If I wasn't so unsure of myself, I would have spoken up*? I have rewritten parts of my life in ways where I came out the victor instead of the victim. I portray myself as the one who didn't back down but rose to the occasion in the defense of integrity and respect for others. In my remake of the story, I am not one to be messed with. But to be completely transparent, I must share the original version of what took place and how it sometimes prevents me from moving forward and letting it go.

I remember being around twelve or thirteen years old when I moved back to London from New York. I went to live

HELP, I'M DEALING WITH TRAUMA

with my sister because I had been acting terribly in school. My mother thought it best that I finish school there and then come back to the States. I didn't want to go back to London but I made the best of it in the hopes of coming back to America.

One day after being in London for a few months, I was in my bedroom when I heard screaming and yelling coming from my sister's room. I thought I was hearing things, so I decided to tune it out and continue people-watching from the window. A few minutes later, however, the screaming became louder, and I began to hear the unmistakable noise of furniture being destroyed. I realized my sister's boyfriend was physically abusing her. I was horrified. I didn't know what to do. I thought about going into the kitchen to get a knife to stab him to death. I thought about kicking in the door like Mr. T would on *The A-Team* and whooping his ass like the punk that he was. Thoughts raced through my head, but I was afraid of what would happen. So, instead, I wrote a note saying "My sister's boyfriend is beating her up" and held it up to the window until someone noticed and called the police.

A few minutes later the police arrived. My sister answered the door. The police informed her there was a report of someone in the house being abused. She lied and said everything was okay. After some convincing, the police finally left.

That night my sister came to my room and we fell asleep together. I was angry I couldn't help her and even more angry that I didn't kill that bastard for harming my sister. The next morning my sister's boyfriend came into the kitchen like nothing ever happened. He tried to strike up a conversation with me, but I was clearly not interested in speaking to him. I had a fork in my hand, and I thought about gouging his eyes out. I wanted him to feel pain like my sister did the night before. Thankfully, my sister and her boyfriend eventually broke up when she finally fought back and kicked him out.

I have been struggling with forgiving myself for not being there for her. Sometimes when I think about her, I think about that day and how I could have prevented the abuse. I start to think, *If only I were strong enough to fight him, he would have never, ever put his hands on her again.* Then I snap out of it and remind myself I was a child and there was really nothing I could do but call the police. In June 2009 my sister passed away from cancer. Not a day goes by that I don't think about her and the things she went through. My version of how I would have liked to deal with her boyfriend is very different from what took place some thirty years ago. The reality, though, is that I cannot go back. I must, therefore, move forward. While I cannot change the past, what I *can* do is think about all the other times I was there for her and be thankful for that.

Don't you dare mess with my mother!

My mother divorced my father circa 1983. They had a rocky relationship from the start, I am told. My father was unfaithful and had quite the temper. My mother is also a bit quick tempered, so they had a tumultuous, short-lived relationship. My mother told me she was warned not to get involved with the man who became my father. Several people warned her he was no good and only after her money and house. My mother even approached him about the things she heard, but naturally, he denied them. My mother told me she saw warning signs but never really took them seriously; she just assumed everything would work out.

I'd like to pause the story here to suggest that if you hear things and notice red flags about someone you're interested in dating, you should consider being cautious about moving forward with that person. At the very least, you may want to explore the health and strength of the relationship before bringing children into the world. Many times, we get caught up in emotions but after the excitement of a fresh relationship wears off, we are left with someone who was only really drawn to what we had or what we could do for them and never really valued us. This can be traumatizing in that we gave our authentic selves to someone who never did the same. Don't ever lose yourself trying to fit into someone else's idea of who you are or *should* be.

So, back to my mother. She once told me that when I was about two years old she and my father got into a nasty argument. As they were going back and forth, my father went to punch her and I jumped off the bed and bit him on the ankle. My dad screamed out and said, "Tris"—referring to my middle name—"even you are against me?!" My response, as I am told, was "You better not touch my mum." As the story goes, he then tried to pick up our television to walk out with it, but I bit him on the ankle again. In my anger I told him to leave our TV alone and get out.

I'm not sure where I got all of that protective energy from, but I am glad it came in handy. I do wish I had that same fire when I realized my sister was being mistreated. Sometimes when you are faced with so much violence and live in fear it can drain your energy and prevent you from stepping into a situation when you are needed. On the other hand, I am glad I was there to defend my mum even though she was more capable of defending herself in that moment.

Shortly after that incident, my father moved out. In a strange order of events, it was my mother who provided him with the down payment to get his own home. Of course, in true fashion, he didn't pay her back. My mother didn't have to loan him the money, but in her kindness and generosity she was still the bigger person. My mother has proven to be a strong woman who has overcome much adversity and trials but through it all she has accomplished much and is still standing.

Are my eyes deceiving me?

Just like any little brother, I always wanted to hang out with my older brother. He had a cool car, dressed real nice, gave us money when we asked, and bought my niece, adopted brother, and me whatever we asked for (within reason). You couldn't tell me anything about my big brother. In my mind he was the best big brother in the whole world. I would spend the weekends at his house and hang out there with my nephew. My nephew and I would play fight with my brother, and he would let us think we could beat him. I really looked up to him. He was my hero. But there is an adage that says, "Never meet your heroes." They will always disappoint you.

One weekend, when I was staying over at my brother's house, I was heading downstairs when I saw the most horrifying thing. I witnessed my hero, my big brother, punching his wife in the face. I had never seen anything like it. When he noticed me standing there, he said, "Tristram, get upstairs, now." I ran back upstairs and jumped back into bed. From that day I never spent the night at his house again. I never shared this story with anyone except my mother and I only did that once I was in my mid-twenties. What I saw that night was devastating. How could someone treat their wife like that? How could a man punch someone in the face? Especially a woman? That night I lost all respect for my brother; I hated him for years. I never wanted anything to do with him, and I made it obvious.

Thankfully his wife divorced him and got away from his abuse. As I got older my relationship with my brother became very strained because I couldn't get over the behavior I had seen from my so-called hero. Several years later he moved with us to the U.S. While living with my mother and I, he bullied me whenever he got the chance. That didn't last long because at that point I was older and no longer afraid. We would get into fistfights. Though I didn't win those fights, I made it known he was not going to take advantage of me because I knew who he really was: an abusive coward.

Over the years the fights got worse, and he eventually moved out. I haven't seen him since my early twenties, and the last time we saw one another, you would have thought it was the WWE Royal Rumble. My mother was thinking of moving to Florida, so my brother invited her down to look at a house. She didn't want to go by herself, so we decided to make a trip out of it. My sister Rae flew in from London with her then-boyfriend, and I, of course, was not about to miss out on a free trip to Florida. Everything was going well; my mother stayed with my brother and his girlfriend and my sister, her boyfriend, and I stayed at a hotel a few miles away. One day while we were at

Miami Beach my brother called me. He wanted my sister and I to come over and have dinner at his place.

The next day we went to my brother's and were greeted by his girlfriend. What was so unusual about the visit is that my brother never came inside to see us. After a few hours of making awkward small talk, I asked for something to drink. My brother's girlfriend told me to help myself to drinks on the patio. As I went outside to get a soda, I turned around only to find my brother sitting on a lawn chair. I asked him why he wasn't inside with the rest of us. He said he preferred to stay outside. To avoid an argument, I didn't ask any more questions. I told him it was good to see him, gave him a hug, and went back inside. A few minutes later my sister, her boyfriend, and I left and went back to the hotel.

On our final day in Florida, we went to pick up our mom from my brother's place on our way to the airport. My sister and her boyfriend stayed in the car while I grabbed my mom's bags. After I put the suitcases in the car, I went back to get my mom but she had gone to the bathroom. My brother was standing in the living room staring me down. I asked him what was wrong. He told me not to ask him any questions. Before I knew it, we started fighting. My mother screamed out, and that got the attention of my sister's boyfriend. He ran inside and tried to break up the fight but couldn't. After the commotion finally died down my brother screamed out to my mother asking why I hate him so much. I told him it was because he beats women and I couldn't stand him.

Everything I wanted to do when my sister's ex-boyfriend was abusing her and when I saw my brother hit my then-sister-in-law came rushing back. I wanted vengeance! I was tired of letting people get away with it. After I told my brother he was a woman-beater, he simply looked at me in disbelief. I reminded him of what he did to his ex-wife and other women. My family eventually convinced me to get in the car and we drove to the airport. I can't remember what we talked about on the way to the airport; all I know is I was mad as hell and wanted to go back and finish him off. I haven't seen or spoken to my brother since.

Each day I pray to let my anger go and forgive him for his actions, and each day I feel a bit stronger. I'm not sure if I will ever see my brother again, but if I do, I hope it will be a cordial meeting.

Friend or no friend, I better not ever find out that you hit a woman!

The majority of people I know are from the church. As a matter of fact, one of my closest friends when I was about twenty-three years old was someone I met at church. To protect his and others' identities, I'll call him Mark. Mark and I had a few things in common: we love God, we enjoy singing in the choir, and most of all, we loved to chase the ladies. We would go on double dates, visit different churches, and go on road trips together. When you saw Mark, you saw me. The only person who knew more about Mark than me was his mother, and even then I think we were neck and neck in that department. Though I knew so much about Mark, there was something troublesome about him that caused our friendship to end abruptly.

Mark dated this wonderful young lady, Michelle. Michelle also attended our church and sang with us in the choir. Mark was not faithful to any of the women he was seeing at the time. I think they were aware of his unfaithfulness but never brought it up. Michelle and Mark dated for quite some time; there was even talk of them getting married. They seemed very happy, and Mark stopped seeing other women, so we thought for sure this was it. One day, Michelle and I were in the choir room with another church friend, Derrick. I'm not sure how we got on the topic of Mark, but we ended up discussing Mark and Michelle's relationship. During that conversation Michelle informed us that Mark had hit her. You can only imagine the rage I felt. I'd already witnessed people I love being abused by their boyfriends and husbands. And now someone I called my closest friend was committing the same egregious act. When Michelle shared this information with us, I was stunned; I was downright pissed. I asked her if she was okay and when the last time was that Mark had hit her. She said it had been a few days prior. I told her we would handle it.

Derrick saw the rage in my eyes. I could not care less what Mark's excuse was. There is no excuse for putting your hands on a woman. When Mark got back to the church, Derrick and I confronted him. We offered to get him help if he needed it. His response shocked us both. He said, "I don't need you guys to Dr. Phil me, and the both of you need to stay out of my business." I became angry and got in his face. Before I could get any words out Derrick jumped in between us. Mark asked if I was going to fight him. I told him that if he put his hands on Michelle again I would.

Needless to say, Michelle and Mark broke up shortly after that. Our friendship also ended. I could no longer be friends with someone who abused women. That is where I draw the line.

I know I cannot go back into the past, but what I can control is my present and my future. Though I wish I had the wisdom and the strength to defend my sister and sister-in-law when I was younger, the fact is that I couldn't. I was too young to understand and too fearful to react appropriately. What I can do is make it my business to intervene when I see it happening. I can do things like notify the police when I see something that is out of the ordinary. Without getting too involved I know I can be there for someone who may not know how to get out of an abusive relationship. I am older, wiser, and stronger to defend those who cannot defend themselves.

Getting over the trauma of your past is not an easy venture. It will take time to fully recover. For me, every time a disturbing memory tries to invade my peace and progress, I remind myself this event has already run its course. There is freedom in knowing you cannot change the past but you can definitely create a better future. When I realized I had the opportunity to be better, I became better. Don't be a prisoner of history that cannot be reshaped. Instead, be the architect of a new beginning.

To all the women who have been abused and found relief, I commend your courage. To those who are being abused, you can get out of that relationship, and you can get help. Refuse to allow anyone to devalue you and strip you of your inner and outer beauty.

To the memory of those who have lost their lives to physical abuse, I wish I could have been there to defend you, yet I know God will bring justice to those who caused you pain. Rest in peace!

2

The Trauma of Grief

I Hate Funerals

I don't think anyone has ever said, "I can't wait to get to that funeral." I think the only folks who look forward to death are morticians. Death is inevitable. We are all going to arrive at that day when our friends and family are going to have to say their final goodbyes to us. While we will be gone, those we leave behind will have to bear the pain of our passing. They will grapple with the reality that we no longer exist in the world and will be left to carry the trauma of grief. There are times I ask God why he took a certain person, why a loved one had to suffer through sickness, why he had to break my heart this way. But while it hurts to lose people we love, that's a part of life we all have to deal with.

I remember when I saw my mother grieve over the passing of her friend, Mr. Benjamin Simmons. I had the daunting task of informing her that he transitioned. Mr. Simmons, as I called him, was a real nice guy. I cannot remember how he and my mother met but they became good friends, and he helped us navigate this new country in the early days of our arriving in the United States. He would drive us around and take my mother food shopping, and when we bought our new home, he helped us find people to decorate. He was a kind and gentle soul.

We didn't know too many people in New York, and the family that we knew were not kind. Also, the folks my mother thought were her friends had hidden agendas and tried to take advantage of her kindness and generosity. So, when Mr. Simmons entered our lives, it was a breath of fresh air.

One day we went to visit some of those people my mom thought were her friends. One Sunday afternoon my mother and I were heading over to their house, and just before we arrived, Mr. Simmons called and asked to speak with my mother. He told my mom the people we were about to visit were not her friends. He said they were always talking about her. He told her to be careful with them. Shortly after that she realized Mr. Simmons was right.

About a year or so later my mother wanted to move into her own home. My mother was already a homeowner in London and wanted to purchase a house in the U.S. She had set money aside to buy a house in an account that had my uncle's name on it (my mother's brother). Unfortunately, my uncle robbed my mother of that money and bought a house of his own. My mother was devastated. She was so upset she contemplated moving back to London.

My mother shared the awful news with Mr. Simmons, and he encouraged her to stay and told her everything would work out. We started looking for a house. We found a great home in Roosevelt, New York, on Denton Place. It had three bedrooms and a living room, dining room, den, basement, and swimming pool and a garage my mother wanted to convert into a bedroom and kitchen. It was a great house, but my uncle had stolen the money my mother would have used for a down payment. I'll talk more about that situation and other family members when we get to the chapter on family trauma.

One day, as my mom was sharing her exasperation over not having the down payment, Mr. Simmons said something that renewed my mother's faith in God and good people. He told her he would loan her the money so she could get the house. My mother was hesitant. She told him she wasn't sure when she would be able to pay him back. Mr. Simmons was a straight shooter and didn't hold back his thoughts. He quickly responded, "I didn't ask you to worry about paying me back; I just want to help you out." After some discussion my mother accepted the funds and was able to buy her home. A few months later my mother was able to pay him back. We were so happy about having our own home in the U.S. and not worrying about living in an apartment or staying with family.

Things were looking up for us, and it seemed we were making great strides in our new home. About a year later, Mr. Simmons came to visit us as he normally would. That particular day, Mr. Simmons didn't seem himself at all. You could tell there was something on his mind. My mother asked him what was wrong. He sighed and shared that he had been diagnosed with bone cancer. My mother screamed out and cried uncontrollably. I was in shock.

Mr. Simmons told my mom there was nothing much the doctors could do. The cancer had spread, and he didn't have much time left. That afternoon we stayed in the kitchen. My mother cooked a traditional West Indian dish called cook-up rice, and we ate like it was the Last Supper. Mr. Simmons was very grateful for the friendship he and my mother had and I know my mother was grateful, as well. As time went on, Mr. Simmons didn't come by as often because he was in and out of the hospital and unable to drive.

Not too long after, Mr. Simmons passed away. Ironically, it was another Saturday afternoon when I received the phone call indicating he had passed. I waited for my mother to get home from work and gave her the gut-wrenching news. My mother cried for hours. Mr. Simmons was a great friend. He had no hidden agendas. He didn't try to get my mother into bed. He wasn't mean to me. He was truly one of the good ones.

Later that week his family held a wake. That would be the first of many wakes and funerals I would attend. The place was packed. There were people gathered outside, and there were blocks of people in cars who had shown up to pay their final respects to a great man. As you can imagine, my mother's cries were among many that filled the air. A tremendous amount of people came out to say farewell to a man who touched so many lives. Unbeknownst to my mother and I, Mr. Simmons was a deacon at Union Baptist Church in Hempstead, New York. What I find so amazing is that he never invited us to church or tried to convert us. What he did was even better. He brought the church to us and showed us what God looks like in human form. Many people get caught up with titles and what they do in God's house, and the truth of the matter is they act more like the devil than Jesus.

Mr. Simmons was the embodiment of Christianity, and he didn't go around bragging about it. He was the type of man who showed his Christianity instead of just talking about it. I have to say I have never met a man like Mr. Simmons since. He was one of a kind and is still missed to this day. My mother and I always reminisce about how he would take us out and treat us with so much respect and dignity. My mother has never had another friend like Mr. Simmons. That type of grief had an impact on both of us. We never really trusted anyone the way we trusted Mr. Simmons. My mother and I have been through a lot together and we helped each other through that grief by just being there for one another. We will never find another man like Deacon Benjamin Simmons. He will forever be in our hearts as a true friend and a true man of God.

Why her? Why now?

My sister Rae is seven years older than I am, and she is one of the reasons I am an avid reader today. She would encourage me to read as many books as possible. At twenty years old, instead of going to parties and hanging out, she loved reading and doing things no one in the family had ever done before. She went to school, obtained her master's degree in psychology, started her own business, and owned several properties in the U.K. Rae was a determined and adventurous woman who refused to allow anyone to hold her down. When she finally got out of that abusive relationship, she finally started to soar.

Things were going in the right direction. She was making moves and making money. In her house you would find fancy clothes, expensive shoes, and lavish furniture, but what was amazing to me is that she had a room dedicated to her collection of books. She never stopped expanding her knowledge. If she didn't know something, she would go buy a book on it and then explain it like she invented it. I really believe reading was her first love. I remember the first book she gave me, Alice Walker's *The Color Purple*. I also remember my response when I saw what I believed to be a monstrosity of a book. I said, "I'm not reading this thick-ass book." She responded, "As long as you're living in my house, your ass is not going to play outside until you have read and given me a verbal report about it." I won't tell you what I thought about that. Needless to say, I read the book and it drove me to want to read and study more. Because of her I have more books than clothes and shoes combined. I am thankful for what she instilled in me about the power of reading and applying what you read to your life. That is life changing.

Maybe twelve years before her death, I remember having a conversation with Rae about her life and where she felt she would be heading. She said something to me that really blew me away. She said, "I don't believe I am going to live very long. It's not meant for me to be here long." I was shocked and confused. She explained, "I just know. But you must live your life and take care of yourself." I will never forget that conversation. I'm not sure how she knew she wouldn't live a long life, but she was right. What I find so interesting is that for the next twelve years or so she did amazing things in her career and traveled to places I dream of and hope to travel to someday as well. Though she knew her time was short, she did not sit around just waiting to die or waiting for something tragic to happen. Instead, she worked hard and played harder. She grew a foster childcare business she had founded, she furthered her education by getting certified in different fields, and she purchased more property to broaden her wealth. Her mind was set on doing as much as she could with the limited time she had. I believe she got that drive from our mother. Rae lived her life and made an impact on many. She, too, was kind and generous. Though she had her faults, as we all do, her compassion overshadowed everything else.

Around 2005 or 2006, Rae complained about pain in her breast. She went to doctors in the U.K. and they told her it was just a cyst. The doctors said they would drain it and she would be fine. The issue resurfaced a year later and she was in unbearable pain. She decided to see a specialist. After rounds of testing, Rae was diagnosed with stage four breast cancer. It had already metastasized. The stinging pain I felt when she shared the news of her diagnosis was the same pain I felt when I realized she was being abused by her boyfriend. And once again there was nothing I could do to help my sister in her time of pain. Again, I was called upon to break this atrocious news to my mother. My mother was still working at the time, and I had driven her to work that day. When I returned to pick her up, she asked me for an update on Rae. I asked her to get in the car first. She refused, demanding I tell her immediately. It was as if she already knew. I put the car in park and begged her to get in the car. She broke down crying. "She has cancer, right?"

After some persuasion, she finally got in the car, and I told her the news. My mother cried all the way home. That night we were on the next flight to London to be with Rae. Neither one of us slept the whole way. We were too busy cycling between anxiety, anger, and heartbreak. When we finally arrived in London we headed straight to Rae's home in Forest Hills. Rae was standing outside to greet us with a great big smile on her face. Through all of her pain she was so happy to see us, and we were overjoyed to see her as well.

Initially we didn't address the elephant in the room, we just enjoyed being in the moment. After a few hours of talking, Rae asked our mom if she was tired. Mom said, "Not really." Rae responded, "Good, do you feel like cooking?" All three of us busted out laughing. Mom said she would make whatever Rae wanted. I can't remember what Mom cooked; all I know is that we devoured it like it was our last meal. All felt right with the world and we made a decision not to talk about her diagnosis until we all went together to see the specialist.

The next day we went to see a doctor. We wanted a second opinion and needed to know what options were available for my sister. The doctor informed us there were several options. One was aggressive chemotherapy, and another was removal of her breast. At this point Rae was very discouraged; she didn't want to lose her breast or her hair because of the chemo. After several days of back and forth, Rae decided to go in another direction. There was a woman in London who claimed to be a holistic healer.

My mother and I were very skeptical about this person and wanted to know more about her experience and who she had helped. We all agreed to go visit her. When we arrived at the healer's home, she asked my mother and I to wait in another room while she talked to Rae by herself. About thirty minutes later, the two of them came out of the other room. We were hoping to hear some hopeful news, but Rae was ready to go. After we got into the car Rae began to tell us all of the ways she would be treated and her decision to go through with the holistic healer. My mother and I were not comfortable with her making that decision by herself, but we agreed to support her decision. A week later I was scheduled to head back to the

States because I needed to look for a job. I made sure my last week in London was stress free for my sister and did my best to enjoy the time we had.

After I arrived back in the U.S., I spoke to Rae at least two to three times a week. My mother stayed in London to support Rae. One day, Rae called while I was home. Before I could finish saying "Hello," she blurted out, "You are not going to believe this!" I could tell by the frustration and anger in her voice that this was not going to be good. I asked her what was wrong. She said she was livid. She asked, "Do you remember the holistic healer I was seeing? Well, she is a fraud! She lied about being a survivor of breast cancer and about her experience in holistic medicine."

Rae was right to be upset. I had no words to comfort my sister. Once again, I was unable to be there for her in the way she needed. I tried to calm her down, but it was of no use. I felt completely helpless; my sister trusted this person to help her through her sickness but instead she took advantage of her. It was bad enough I had to leave Rae during her health issue, then to hear this unfortunate news was very frustrating.

As time went on, the cancer continued to spread. I tried to convince her to take the chemo and not to worry about her hair, but Rae refused. So, I did the only thing I could do. I prayed and continued to encourage my sister. Six months later, Rae heard of a specialist in Mexico known for their intense chemotherapy treatments. Rae being Rae made up her mind that she was going to Mexico. My mother went with her. They stayed in Mexico for almost a month.

Unfortunately, Rae got worse. She started throwing up blood and lost a tremendous amount of weight. My mother called from Mexico one day and said, "We almost lost her today." I asked what happened and she explained Rae had passed out from throwing up so much blood. They had to rush her to the hospital.

A week later Rae and my mother returned to New York. When I picked them up from the airport, I barely recognized my sister. This beautiful woman with long hair, a fit body, and a wonderful smile was nothing but skin and bones. I held back tears to try to stay strong for my family. Once we arrived back home, my mother pulled me aside and we cried for a moment together.

Several days later Rae wanted to go back to London. I remember that night when I drove her and my mother back to the airport. Rae pulled me aside and said with a big smile on her face, "I'm going to miss your big head." I held back tears and told her, "I'm going to miss you too, fathead." We both laughed and hugged. That was the last time I ever held my sister in my arms.

Two weeks later, on a Saturday evening, Rae called. I thought it was my mother calling with awful news, but it was Rae. I was relieved to hear her voice. She said, "Tris, I am going to die, and I am ready to go." For several minutes I cried uncontrollably. I cried until my eyes were sore. After I gathered myself, I said, "Let's pray about this." She responded, "I don't want to pray anymore. I'm in pain and there has got to be a better place than this." She told me she needed me to be strong and take care of our mom.

We said "I love you" to each other and hung up. I didn't sleep that night. The next day I called to speak to my mother, and as soon as she answered, I burst into tears. Rae got on the phone and tried to calm me down, but I couldn't stop crying. After some time I was able to get it together. I was scheduled to fly to Denver that evening for a work trip. I started to cancel the flight, but my sister insisted I go and encouraged me to give a great presentation for work. For that entire week all I could do was think of her.

That Sunday was the last time I spoke to Rae. Her condition got worse, and she was too weak to talk. One Tuesday in June my mother called and said Rae had stopped eating and talking. Mom asked me how soon I could get to London. I told her I would be there by Friday. Friday morning, I arrived at Heathrow Airport and headed straight to the hospital. Rae was unrecognizable. She had lost so much weight, and her breathing was faint. When I arrived in her room, I held her feet gently because she was in so much pain. I told her, "I am here now; you are free to go." At 5 p.m. on Saturday, June 20, 2009, Rae Samantha Bishop took her final breath. On Friday, July 10, we said farewell.

I have not been able to fully grieve her death because I had to handle the funeral arrangements, write the obituary, and eulogize her. I guess I could say I'm still in shock. I'm still heartbroken. But I keep moving forward. That's the thing about grief, you never fully get over losing someone you love. You just learn how to adapt to the pain. That is exactly what I have done. I've adapted to the pain, just hoping one day the pain will subside. It was not easy adjusting. It was like I had to rewire my brain, and when I thought about Rae, I made sure I reminisced on the wonderful times we shared. It sounds very simplistic, yet it's extremely helpful, especially when the anniversaries of her death and birthday roll around. I don't think my mother has fully recovered either. We try not to talk about Rae's death much because it hurts too bad. Instead, we do our best to remember the good times.

Rae was very involved in the community; her nonprofit agency where she catered to foster children received national attention. She was also nominated for an award for her contributions to foster care. There were so many people who admired her work ethic, leadership, tenacity, and commitment to the foster children in her care. I still remember the funeral, the horse-drawn carriage that carried her body to her final resting place. Hundreds of people showed up for her final farewell. I just hope I made her proud by making sure she was celebrated appropriately.

I can't take any more of this!

One person who would buy me anything no matter what was my oldest sister, Deborah. She was the type of big sister that if I said I wanted a pony, she would work it out and get me a pony. I don't know why she was so generous; she didn't have much, but she had a huge heart. When we moved to the U.S. in 1987, I didn't get to see much of my siblings or other family members in London as often as I would have liked. I missed them terribly. So, whenever they would say they were coming to America for vacation I would be over-the-moon ecstatic about their upcoming visit. When you are living alone with your mother with no other siblings around you can get bored and lonely. Don't get me wrong; my mom is great, but she worked all the time to provide for me and I was at home a lot by myself. So, a visit from my siblings was the highlight of my year. Those were some great times when Rae, Deborah, and my niece Little Rae (Deborah's daughter) would come and visit. We would travel to Manhattan and just take in all the sights. Whatever NYC had to offer, we were right there every day enjoying it to the fullest. Those memories linger on in my heart.

As time went on Deborah and I didn't stay in touch as often as Rae and I did. We just grew apart. We never had a falling out, never really had a disagreement; we just didn't keep in touch the way we were supposed to.

As a result of estranged relationships, Deborah and I had minimal contact. Whenever I would visit London as I grew older, I wouldn't see her much even though I would be there for several weeks at a time. I'm not sure if she was avoiding me or not. All I know is I would be in London for two months at a time and only see her briefly while there. I tried not to read too much into it but couldn't help but feel that she wasn't spending time with me on purpose. As years went by, I may have seen Deborah once every five or six years.

Fast-forward to June 2009; Rae had been gone for a few days and I was preparing for her funeral. I went to Deborah's house to let her know what was happening. She wasn't home when I arrived, but my niece Little Rae was. I asked her to call her mother for me. We spoke on the phone, and she was obviously upset about our sister's passing. I told Deborah I was looking forward to seeing her, even though I wished it was under better circumstances. Her response was disturbing. She said, "I'll see if I can work that out." Caught off guard, I reiterated that I wanted to see her and tried to confirm she would be at the funeral. She explained she wasn't sure if she would be at the funeral because she didn't want to see "that woman." I didn't know what woman she was referring to. Turns out she meant our mother. In my family we often are and must be deliberately direct with each other to communicate our point of view. When I retorted that she and our mother needed to squash this beef and come together on this, she ended the call abruptly.

The day came for Rae's funeral, and among all of the people who showed up I did not see my sister Deborah. A week after Rae's funeral I received a call from my aunt informing me that Deborah was upset with me. She said I walked right passed her as I was heading to the cemetery after Rae's service. I knew that was impossible because if I had seen her, I would have embraced her and spoken. The truth of the matter was Deborah was avoiding me and our mother. After all of that I never did see my sister.

It's really unfortunate that members of my family don't know how to deal with their emotions or whatever is affecting their communication with one another. They would rather not speak to you for the rest of their life and then have the nerve to cry when you die. In reality they could've acted like adults and confronted the situation respectfully. That's the shit that I've never been able to come to grips with. Deborah had an opportunity to rectify a long-standing feud with our mother; however, because of how all of us were raised, that never happened. My mother also had the same opportunity, but because of her own upbringing, that was not going to happen. There are times when I find myself being upset with how everything went down between my mother and the rest of my siblings. The thing is, when you have been surrounded by people who are toxic and refuse to change, they can have a harmful impact on how you interact with people. My family members are stubborn, always have been. I just hope the next generation will have the strength to break this vicious cycle.

December 2010 came around and my wife, Kim, and I were living in a two-bedroom apartment in Mount Vernon. One morning I woke up and told Kim I was going to reach out to Deborah because I would hate it if anything ever happened to her and I didn't get to see her. I called my Aunt Ursela to get Deborah's number. My aunt told me she was not comfortable giving me her number. I started to curse her out, as my mother's family has a history of being secretive and withholding pertinent information. Some of them think it's a game, when in fact it is toxic, hurtful, and manipulative. But I was trying to be a better person. I tried to stay calm. I asked her to give Deborah my number and tell her to call me because I would love to speak with her. My aunt assured me she would, but I never did receive that phone call.

For about a year and a half, I thought constantly about Deborah and prayed for her but was unable to connect with her by phone. As time went on, I could never shake the notion that something was wrong but I could never figure out what it was. Looking back, I think I should have been more aggressive in my pursuit to reestablish a relationship with my only surviving sister. She also could have made an effort to contact me. Neither of us did enough.

During this time in life, every first full week in June I attend the Hampton University Ministers' Conference in Virginia. June 2012 was no exception. By this time, I worked for *Guideposts* magazine, and part of my job was to recruit pastors and their churches to be prayer partners with the ministry and train their members to be prayer volunteers for our prayer line. I was on my way to Hampton but I was a little on edge because Kim and I just had our second child, Sasha, born just a few weeks earlier, so it was hard leaving them. I kept getting an uneasy feeling that something was wrong. I called Kim and my mother constantly to make sure they were okay, and they assured me everything was fine and there was no need to worry. I went on about my week the best I could, but I couldn't shake the feeling that something wasn't right. The week at Hampton went well, and by Friday morning I was heading home. I was excited to see my family and especially our newborn, Sasha.

That Saturday morning, I was home with the family and my mother was back at her house in Roosevelt. All morning I had no appetite and felt strange. Around noon my phone rang. It was my Aunt Ursela from London. She asked me how everyone was and how I was doing and if Sasha was okay. She then asked if my mother was still with us. I said she had returned home and then asked her what was going on. That's when she told me Deborah had died. I said, "Deborah who?" She said, "Deborah your sister." I dropped the phone and fell to my knees crying. Kimberlee came running to see what was wrong. I could barely breathe and was crying hysterically. I could not believe the only two sisters I had were gone. To this day I can't even really describe all of the emotions I felt and still feel. The gut-wrenching pain tore me to pieces. I couldn't speak. After a few minutes I was able to regain my composure. I asked my aunt what had happened. My aunt informed me that Deborah had breast cancer. I couldn't believe it. Deborah was battling breast cancer at the same time Rae was.

Then I figured it out. She didn't want to see me because I would have recognized she was sick too. My aunt continued and told me it had been a tough six months for her, "especially after the boy died." I didn't know what boy she was talking about. She explained, "the boy, Deborah's brother." I was completely confused. I have two brothers, Patrick and my half-brother Karl, and I didn't know what my aunt meant. I asked, "Patrick is dead?" She responded, "No, her father's son." I yelled out, "Karl is dead?!" Apparently, he had died in January. I dropped the phone again and screamed. How is it that I didn't know my adopted brother died and that my last living sister had cancer? I was a complete wreck. I asked my aunt if she knew Deborah was sick. She did. I pushed further and asked why my aunt hadn't told me and my mother. She responded that Deborah didn't want us to know.

I went from being in pain to being enraged at my aunt and other family members who knew and didn't say a word. Then my aunt asked me a stupid question. She asked if I was going to tell my mother. I asked why I would keep this news from her. I told her I was heading to my mother's house that moment. Before I hung up, I asked when Deborah had died. She said, "Wednesday, June fifth." That was the week I was in Hampton and couldn't figure out why I was on edge.

I hung up the phone and went to see my mother. Once again, I was left to bring devastating news to her. The ninety-minute drive felt like an eternity, but I made it. I was concerned she would be so shocked by the news she would have a heart attack. When I got to my mother's house, I told her I was just there to check on her. We headed upstairs to her bedroom, and as she sat on the bed eating ice cream, I stood there wondering how I was going to say this. Mom, sensing something was up, asked what was wrong. I told her I had to tell her something and sat down next to her and told her Deborah died. She asked, "Deborah who?" I said, "Deborah your daughter." My mother looked at me and the tears began to flow. She became a complete wreck. I couldn't console her. It was too much to bear. We were both distraught. Then I broke the news that Karl had also passed away. The impact of all that had happened, and so suddenly, had us in a whirlwind. I explained what happened and how her sisters knew and didn't tell us. All of that really hurt my mother and I. We were struggling with so many emotions, we didn't know where to begin. To add further insult to injury, Deborah's daughter, my niece Little Rae, had the funeral without us. They buried my mother's child without us knowing. Neither of us got the opportunity to grieve correctly.

These traumatic events had a great deal of impact on my life. As a Christian, I know it is important to forgive. Not for them, but for me. The truth is I haven't truly forgiven my niece and other family members for what they did to my mother. It is hard to conceptualize how it feels for a parent to bury a child; it is even more difficult to imagine burying more than one. Then to deny that parent the right to grieve is absolutely appalling. So, while my pain is valid, as time goes on, I want to be free of that animosity toward my family. I wish I could have spent more time with Deborah. Unfortunately, that time never came. I cannot speak on behalf of my mother, but I know she has some regrets as well, especially when her and Deborah's relationship was so strained. Sadly, there is nothing we can do about any of that now. Not being able to connect with Deborah before her passing and, to add insult to injury, not having the opportunity to be involved with her funeral has been very traumatic. I wish I could share a lesson or takeaway that I've learned from this experience, but I can't. It wouldn't be authentic. What I can share is that this experience has left me shattered without any closure. All I can say here is try to do your best to live as well as possible with your family and friends. You never know what tomorrow may bring. We have to move on and be at peace with what God allows. Rest in peace, Deborah Patricia Whall Roberts.

I have mixed emotions

Since the age of nine I can count on one hand the number of times I saw my father. As I shared previously, my mother and father divorced around 1983. He would come by and pick me up and I would spend some weekends with him. From what I can remember they were fun times. As I mentioned, in 1986, my mother, Rae, and I moved to the U.S. My mother wanted a better life for us and she believed America was where she would find that. It was a culture shock. There were cars driving on the other side of the road, funny accents, and the food just didn't quite taste the same. It was a major adjustment. In the midst of all of that, not only did I miss my family, I missed the weekends I would spend with my dad. My parents didn't have the best relationship, and I was caught in the middle. My mother no longer wanted to stay in London, and my father didn't want her to take me away. It was a big mess. There were times when things were done out of spite and not in my best interests.

I was being used as a tool of manipulation and all that did was add more trauma to my life. My parents no longer had my best interests in mind; they were more concerned with hurting one another than protecting me. This was no good for me because all they did was tear one another down whenever I was with either one of them. My dad would call my mother terrible names and my mother would express her disgust for her soon-to-be ex-husband. Truthfully speaking, I was sick of them both. I was tired of them telling me how much they despised one another. I had had enough of the bickering; it affected my sleeping and eating habits. It was too much for me to handle at such a young age.

I was in the middle of my parent's messy divorce, and the custody battle was even worse. Between the ages of nine and fourteen I would visit London quite often and I would make sure to spend time with my dad, but it wasn't the same. He was cold and distant and only wanted to talk about how much he despised my mother. After a while I didn't want to hear it, so instead of being disrespectful, I would just cut the visits short. There were times I would call him and try to have a conversation, but those calls lasted only a few minutes. I would ask him to give me a call when he could, but he never did.

Over time, my relationship with my dad became nonexistent. Years would go by and we wouldn't speak. My mother would suggest I check on my father. For a long time, I blamed both of them for their actions and for putting me in the middle of their problems. After a while I came to terms with the reality that my father would not play a major role in my life. Understanding the impact his absence has had on my life, I have chosen to take that trauma and use it as fuel. As a result, I am even more committed to being involved in every aspect of my children's lives. Kimberlee and I have no plans or desires to divorce, but in the awful event that we did, I would make sure I still showed up for my children as a present and loving father.

As I got older, I didn't visit London as much and therefore saw my father even less. One of my last visits before he was diagnosed with dementia was fairly unpleasant. He still wanted to bring up stuff that had happened decades ago and complained that I'd never brought him a gift from the U.S. That really bothered me because he had long ago made sure to stop paying child support once my mother decided to leave the country. He was trying to hurt her, but in reality, he was avoiding his responsibilities as a father. Needless to say, I cut that visit short. I had tried to establish a relationship with my dad, but I don't think he was interested. I still tried to reach out to him on holidays, but those calls never lasted long.

I'll never forget when Kimberlee and I were planning our wedding and I called my dad to invite him. I believe I had also previously sent him an invitation in the mail. Several months before the wedding I reached out to ask if he would come. He said, "No, I won't be able to make it. I'll catch your next one." My next one? I was only planning on getting married once. I tried to convince him to come and meet his grandson, who had recently been born, but he refused. I was crushed. It seemed every time I extended an olive branch it was smacked out of my hand. It was hard for me to deal with the fact that my father was alive and well and refused to celebrate a great moment in my life.

I would speak to my dad once a year on Christmas morning until the Alzheimer's grew significantly worse and he was unable to speak. The last time I saw my father alive was the spring of 2014. At that time, he was unable to speak, so I just sat with him while he stared out the window of his bedroom. After that visit I would keep in contact with my stepmother, Patsy, who would keep me up to date on his progress. Patsy passed away in 2016. Before she died, she put my father in a nursing home because she was in the hospital. There was no one else to care for him in London and that was the best choice. I would speak to the nurses once a week about my father's condition and they assured me he was well taken care of.

On Sunday, January 21, 2018, I was sitting in the pulpit at church getting ready to preach the morning message. The choir was wrapping up their final song and I was opening my iPad to locate the introduction of my sermon. As I was pulling up the message, an email popped up from my cousin in London. It read:

> Hello Tristram,
> Your father passed away today. I went to warm up his food and when I got back he was gone. Carer Ali said he must have just passed away. Gave him hugs and kisses, told him I know Patsy was there waiting for him. He died in his bed warm and comfortable with no pain.
> Sonia

At that moment the choir was making their way back to the choir stand and I was sitting there in disbelief. I took a deep breath, stood, and started preaching. I had no time to cry or react. I just preached the gospel of Jesus Christ. It looks like I am always forced to deal with pain and grief without ever having a moment to gather my thoughts or to process what has taken place. Death is like that. You don't really get a warning unless you really know a person is about to slip away, and even then, you are still caught off guard. After I preached the sermon and offered salvation to those who may not have had a relationship with Christ, I informed the church of what happened.

The congregation was very supportive and understood I needed time to see about my father's affairs.

The coming weeks are hard to describe. There were days I was dealing with the loss, then there were days it felt like a dark cloud was over me and refused to let light shine through. I was paralyzed by my grief and I didn't know how to handle it. Whatever chance there was to have a relationship with my dad was gone. I kept wondering if I had tried harder if maybe we could have had a relationship; maybe if he had tried harder it could've worked. So many things were going through my head it sent me into a deep depression. I've never really talked about how I felt when my dad died. I had a hard time explaining my true feelings, and the daily panic attacks didn't help either. I suppressed what I was feeling so I wouldn't burden anyone. In the end, all that did was set me back mentally.

Suppressing how I felt about my dad and his passing sent me into a real low place. I had a hard time functioning at home or at the church where I served as pastor. When I think about it, I was easily irritated, angry, disappointed, and lonely. At that time, I had no one to really talk to about my true feelings. I did not want to talk to my mother about it and I wasn't comfortable talking to my wife. I kept it in, and to this day, I truly haven't discussed it with anyone. It's kind of how I'm wired. It's how I process, and when I'm ready I will release it either to my therapist or in some other way. Some may consider that unhealthy; however, to get through pain you sometimes have to wait and find the right time and place for you to release it.

On Tuesday, February 13, 2018, I laid my father to rest. Mr. Vincent Roy Blackett was no more. As the graveyard workers lowered his body into the earth, I just stood there wishing I had a better relationship with my dad. I couldn't understand why I wasn't afforded the opportunity to have fond memories of my father. I was angry, sad, depressed, and most of all hurt that I couldn't have what others did, which was a true father-and-son relationship. As people started to leave the funeral I stood there in the rain until someone yelled for me to get out of the rain. That was indeed my second worse trip to London. Rae's death was the first and now my father's. I couldn't wait to get back home to my wife and children. I needed some normalcy. I needed to see my children laugh and play. I needed to hold my wife. I needed some joy.

I haven't returned to London since my dad's death. I feel like every time I go there it's never for anything good. Eventually I will go back to put flowers on my sister's and father's graves and show my children and wife around, but as of right now, I have no desire to go. The death of a loved one can really take its toll on you mentally, physically, and spiritually. The trauma of death can prevent you from moving forward and living your life to the fullest. If you let it, death can rob you of your joy and have a negative impact on how you deal with people who come into your life. The aftershocks of death can paralyze you from accepting true love and friendship. It can debilitate your capacity to receive genuine love. Whatever you do, don't let the emotional cycles of life keep you from enjoying the beauty of life. I recommend you live life and live it to the fullest.

That's how I can navigate life after dealing with so much death. I live. When I think about the people I have loved who are now gone, it is a reminder to embrace life and all of its challenges. I don't think you ever get over the death of a loved one. There are times I struggle with their absence. To be honest, it has been a difficult journey. I tried to deal with it on my own, and all that did was lead me to drink. Then one day I realized I had to stop suppressing how I felt, so I took time to grieve. I cried, screamed, lifted weights, went for runs, and sought out a therapist. I did what was necessary so I could finally accept what had happened and move on. Death is inevitable; we will all have to deal with the death of a loved one. The trick is to never let death deteriorate the life you have left. Live, my friend. Live.

3

The Trauma of Family

I Can't Believe I'm Related to Someone Like You

You've heard that old idiom: you can choose your friends, but you can't choose your family. If you are like me, there are times when you look at certain family members and think, *I don't know how you and I are related*. Sometimes family dynamics look great from the outside, but then peek behind the curtain and your opinion changes.

I remember speaking with the babysitter for Brendan, my oldest son. I was impressed by the way she and her sisters interacted with each other. One day I asked the three sisters how it is that they all get along so well. They looked at me and laughed. One sister said, "Lem, let me tell you something, son, we don't always see eye to eye, but we make it our business not to let it fester. When things are weighing heavy on our mind, we don't get an attitude with one another. We call each other to the carpet and lay everything out without excluding anyone." She went on, "After we get to the bottom of the issue, we fix it and move on. What is important is that we don't bring it up again. Once we have discussed it, we move on. There is no need in bringing up the same old stuff when you've already agreed to let it go." She added, "It's important you don't give space for anger and bitterness to grow. Deal with the issue, say what you need to say in a respectable manner, and squash it." They made clear that not everything is resolved in a single conversation. Sometimes it took several conversations for everyone to be on the same page.

I was so impressed by the way they so candidly spoke about how they deal with one another. They also shared that it didn't happen overnight. It took time for them to figure out what works best and was healthiest for their family. Once they were able to lay out the ground rules, everything else fell right into place. I appreciated their transparency.

Having a healthy family is so necessary. You never know from one day to the next if you will be able to embrace or converse with family members again. Family is truly all you have; even God instituted the family before he created the church. Family is God's gift. So why do we treat our family members so badly? Why do we try to sabotage their ability to move ahead? Why do we intentionally harm the ones we love? I don't have all the answers. All I can do is share with you in this book how I survived my family and didn't allow the poison and dysfunction of my birth family to puncture the family I have created with my wife.

This has nothing to do with me

There is a story in the Bible in Genesis 4:1–11 (ESV):

> Now Adam knew Eve his wife, and she conceived and bore Cain, saying, "I have gotten a man with the help of the LORD." And again, she bore his brother Abel. Now Abel was a keeper of sheep, and Cain a worker of the ground. In the course of time Cain brought to the LORD an offering of the fruit of the ground, and Abel also brought of the firstborn of his flock and of their fat portions. And the LORD had regard for Abel and his offering, but for Cain and his offering he had no regard. So Cain was very angry, and his face fell. The LORD said to Cain, "Why are you angry, and why has your face fallen? If you do well, will you not be accepted? And if you do not do well, sin is crouching at the door. Its desire is contrary to you, but you must rule over it."

> Cain spoke to Abel his brother. And when they were in the field, Cain rose up against his brother Abel and killed him. Then the LORD said to Cain, "Where is Abel your brother?" He said, "I do not know; am I my brother's keeper?" And the LORD said, "What have you done? The voice of your brother's blood is crying to me from

the ground. And now you are cursed from the ground, which has opened its mouth to receive your brother's blood from your hand.

This biblical story is recorded as the first murder to ever take place. How interesting it is that it was not between strangers or archenemies. It was between two people who shared the same bloodline. What is so unfortunate is that this would not be the last time family members would kill one another. Throughout history family members have sought to undercut each other for position, money, sex, power, and land. Nothing has been off limits. In the Bible lesson we have an up-close view of the first-ever sibling rivalry. Cain was the oldest and was supposed to know better. Abel was the youngest but had a vast knowledge on how to present his best to God.

The biblical text does not reveal that there was fighting between the brothers growing up. It does not suggest issues of favoritism between their parents, Adam and Eve. What the text does show is that Cain had a deep-rooted animosity toward his brother that had little to do with Abel. Cain disregarded his role of worshipping God correctly. If you thoroughly examine the text, you will see this was probably not the first time Cain brought an offering to the Lord. Cain knew what would be acceptable and what would be rejected. Once Abel brought his offering to God, it somehow outshined Cain's offering. While Cain did not give from his initial harvest, Able gave the first born of his flock. Cain gave God his leftovers. Able presented his very best. Cain's offering was an afterthought and that insulted God. So God rejected Cain's lack of effort and praised Abel's determination to go above and beyond. This set in motion a premeditated homicide that took place on the grounds of the family business.

Abel didn't reject Cain's offering, God did. God even took the necessary steps to warn Cain of his reckless behavior. But instead of listening to God, Cain took his rejection from God out on his brother.

How many times have we been upset with our parents or even a supervisor at work and, instead of resolving the issue with the one responsible, we took that energy and wasted it on blaming someone else? Doing this only hurts us more. In the biblical text, once Cain killed his brother, he was estranged from his parents and God banished him to another part of the world. All of this happened because one family member couldn't check his ego and face his problems like an adult.

I am convinced that was the issue with my siblings. There were things that took place before we were born and because of these relationships that were permanently severed based upon irreconcilable differences, sibling rivalry entered the scene. I've shared memories of my sister Rae. But there is another side to that coin. There were arguments and knock-down drag-out fights. There were moments when we went toe to toe. Neither one of us backed down, so my mother would have to intervene. Many times, if not all of the time, my mom took Rae's side. That infuriated me. I would be so angry at both of them that I needed to go for a long walk before I ended up doing something I would later regret.

As we got older the fights got more intense. I remember a time when I was a teenager and wasn't doing so well in school. My sister called to see how my mother was doing and my mother, in her frustration, would tell Rae about what was going on with me. After my mother and Rae would talk, I would speak to Rae and she would berate me over the phone. One day Rae picked the wrong time to chastise me. I can't quite remember how it all went down. All I remember is that at one point she said, "Don't make me have to come out there to deal with your stupid ass." Why did she have to say that? I was overcome with rage. I told her she could come but would get her ass beat because I wasn't the one to fuck with that day. I cursed her out and then hung up the phone. I looked at my mother and told her to leave me alone. Then I walked out.

I have to admit my relationship with two of my three full siblings has, at times, been fairly turbulent. Truthfully speaking, my mother instigated many of those fights. I've long forgiven her, but it has not been easy to forget. There were times where I blamed my mother for most of the division that took place among my siblings. As I got older, I blamed my siblings and myself that we didn't take the opportunity to make things right. When you are a child, you rely heavily on your parents to prevent division from creeping in between your siblings. When you become adults, that responsibility falls solely on you.

My mother had four children. The two oldest were from her first husband and the last two from her two other husbands. Some of my siblings would blame the new man for interfering in the relationship. One sibling would say, "If your dad didn't come along, my dad would still be married to Mom." Since I am the youngest, I didn't have a younger sibling to blame for my parents' divorce.

The thing is, my mother's relationships had nothing to do with me or my siblings. The issue was that our parents brought us children into adult conversations and that caused a strenuous relationship between us siblings. The contention between Rae and I lasted up to about two years before her death, but the underlying issues had nothing to do with us but with our parents and their lack of communication. I remember when I was putting together Rae's funeral program. I used her computer, and in my searching through files to gather information for the obituary, I stumbled across a letter she wrote to her therapist. Her words were hurtful but honest. In her letter she wrote of her arduous relationship with our mother and her artificial relationship with me. She wrote that she didn't get along well with her mother and that she blamed her for the relationship with her dad not working out. She continued to say that she didn't really like her mother but loved her anyway. What she wrote about me was an eye-opener. She said she did not like me and that she only tolerated me to be polite.

You can only imagine how I felt. I was putting her obituary together and stumbled across awful things she said about me and our mother. What hurt the most was that the letter was written several months before her death.

My brother is the oldest of us four. The fights between him and me escalated quickly every time we would come in contact with one another. I would try to ignore what I heard and knew about him, but then he would prove me and everyone else right through his actions. The relationship between my mother, brother, and my oldest sister was strained from years ago and that trickled down to me and my brother. My oldest sister, Deborah, and I never had a cross word; we just drifted apart.

On the other hand, my brother Patrick and I seemed to get into it no matter what. Fights often erupted from me defending our mother from his attempts to assassinate her character and hold grudges against her for things that happened even before I was born. When he did that I would remind him I hadn't even been born yet and his issues with our mother had nothing to do with me. I would tell him he needed to fix things with our mother and stop allowing their issues to drag him further into bitterness. Although we know how our mother can be, there was no need to keep dwelling on the past.

The same goes for our mother. Some years ago, when my mother was divorcing her first husband, they went to court to see who would gain full custody of the children. My mother's first husband influenced Patrick and Deborah to speak ill of my mother in front of the judge. He told them to tell the judge she didn't take care of them, let them play, or hang out with their friends. They spoke so badly of our mother that she lost full custody and was given six months to move out of a house she bought. This incident caused my mother so much pain. She was distraught and heartbroken. My mother has shared this story with me numerous times, and that leads me to believe that after all these years she has had a hard time getting over what her children did to her. I believe that put an enormous strain on their relationship, which, again, eventually trickled down to me.

It gets deeper! When we first moved to the U.S., we were living with my uncle, the one who ultimately robbed my mother of her money. My mother was maintaining her mortgage on the house in London. A few years later my mother was able to finish paying off her home in London. My mother sent Rae to retrieve the deed from the bank and put it in a safe-deposit box. When Rae arrived at the bank, she was met with some troublesome news. The bank manager informed my sister that she could not retrieve the deed because my mother had not finished paying off the mortgage. My sister presented the letter saying the home was fully paid for. The manager said the first mortgage was finished but the second mortgage was not. Rae was confused and headed home to call my mother. My mother said there was no second. Rae went back to the bank the next day and explained there was no other mortgage. The bank manager then gave Rae a copy of the mortgage agreement. Rae sent the agreement to my mother. When mom and I looked at the date when the second mortgage was taken out, we weren't even in London on that day and the signature on the form was not my mother's. After a few weeks of investigation, we find out that Patrick and Deborah had remortgaged our mother's house. My mother was absolutely dumbfounded. She couldn't believe her children would do such a horrific thing.

When Mom and I moved to the U.S., Rae came along but didn't like it, so she returned to London. Since Rae was only a teenager at the time, Mom put Deborah's and Patrick's names on her accounts in the event of an emergency. So they had access to personal information that gave them the ability to take out an unauthorized, second mortgage.

After about a year in court and my mother proving the signature was not hers, the bank finally released the deed. My mother wanted nothing to do with Deborah or Patrick after that. My mother never saw Deborah after that. We've seen Patrick from time to time, but those interactions have never gone well. Because of what took place, that caused Deborah and I to drift further apart.

For some reason Patrick was able to weasel his way back into my mother's life and manipulate her to put her name on trucks, vans, and even a house in Virginia. I believe my mother did this out of the kindness of her heart because she believed Patrick had changed. My mother was unable to see who he really is, and that caused much pain and resentment among her children. It seemed every time Patrick would slither back into town, I would be the one to clean up the mess by contacting attorneys, helping my mother pay off debt, and selling off a house she never wanted to buy in the first place.

We haven't seen Patrick in a long time. I'm not sure if he is dead or alive. This trauma my mother went through with my two older siblings really took a toll on her. I'm not sure if she has forgiven them for their actions, especially since she speaks of it quite often, regularly finding a way to weave in what she went through with Deborah and Patrick.

Continuous trauma can do that to you if you don't deal with the initial trauma. My mom is old school; she doesn't talk about feelings, and she sure as hell won't see a therapist. So I just try to help her through her pain by being there for her. I would not advise anyone to ignore their feelings, especially when it has caused so much pain. Seeking help for your mental health is necessary and it can prevent long-term damage to you and the relationships you have. Sometimes that's what people need; they need you to be there for them. They may not understand all of the techniques and mental health jargon that we use to help us through our trauma. However, your presence can be calming and reassuring that things will get better.

This shit is in the bloodline

One morning I was out running at the track. My wife sent me a YouTube video filled with motivational talks. As I was putting some miles in, one of the motivational speakers said something that triggered my soul. He said, "It's sad to say, but it's your family and friends that always want to talk you out of your dreams. They are normally the ones to discourage you or are even bold enough to stop you from pursuing your dreams. It's like they become relentless about putting a stop to the vision you have in mind for your life." I think it's awful that in most instances it's rare to have family completely support your efforts.

My mother shared with me that when she bought her second house in London, she had to add her brother Neville's name to the deed because in those times they didn't allow women to obtain mortgages. Before she would add his name, Neville had to sign an agreement that when the mortgage was paid in full he would remove his name from the deed.

Once my mother resolved the issue with the forged second deed, my mother wanted her brother's name off the deed. My mom asked Rae to go to Uncle Neville's house and ask him to sign the paperwork to have his name removed. Rae went to speak to Uncle Neville but he said he was busy and told her to return the next day. When Rae went back the next day, Uncle Neville said he was on his way out so she would have to return another time. This went on for several days. Uncle Neville knew what he was doing; he wanted to keep his name on the deed because he knew the house's value. After several days of going back and forth, Mom told Rae to go back and not to leave until Neville signed the form. My sister went back and did what she was told. Uncle Neville continued to hem and haw. He went to the store. He went to work. When he arrived home, Rae was still there. She told him he needed to sign the form. Instead of signing the form, he took a bath and had dinner. After a few more hours he finally signed the form and Rae left. As she was walking out of the house, Uncle Neville yelled out, "Your mother won't survive in America" and he slammed the door.

It downright sickens me when I hear my mother share these awful stories. I get so upset because I want to know what possesses a person to be so evil. What has overcome them in such a way that they become so dreadful to their own sibling? The only thing that comes to mind is jealousy. Jealousy has ruined friendships, marriages, and business partnerships. Jealousy led my Uncle Neville to covet a home that he didn't invest in. He was blinded by his greed and bound by his own bitterness.

Thankfully my mother didn't allow the resentment my uncle had for her to stop her from climbing higher. I admire my mother's tenacity to keep moving forward in the face of adversity.

The ups and downs of jolly old England

In the late fifties and early sixties, London was the place to move to if you were from either Guyana, Jamaica, or Barbados. Since all of those places were under British rule at the time, it was easy to move, get a job, and start a new life. My mother's other brother, Mansford, was one of the first to move to London. Two days before Uncle Mansford was to move to London, he was short some money for the fare. He went to my mother and asked her for help. My mother, being the generous person she is, gave him the money so he could follow his dreams. After he arrived in London, he wrote my mother every week and encouraged her to come and start a new life. My mother's first husband was already there working and refused to give her money to come to London. She was stuck until my uncle offered to pay for her ticket to get on the ship. Several weeks before my mother left, my Uncle Neville began writing letters to London, telling Mansford not to help my mom. Mansford told my mother all that Neville was saying but she never let that distract her from her goal of starting a new life in London.

My mother stayed with Mansford when she first arrived in London. Upon her arrival, Mansford told her she needed to pay him back for the money he sent for her fare to London. Even though he never paid her back for helping him get to London, he insisted she pay him back. My mother agreed to pay him back once she started working. The next day my mother began to look for work and found a new job in a dry cleaner. She worked the whole day into the evening. When she arrived home, my uncle asked her where she had been all day. She told him she had gotten a job. My uncle was shocked she had gotten a job so quickly.

My mother started to buy kitchen supplies and other items. She also started paying Mansford back and saving money. My mother was on a roll and was feeling good about her future.

One Saturday evening my Uncle Mansford suggested that he and Mom go to a party in the city. My mother had been working for several weeks and decided to go. When they arrived at the party my uncle offered to buy my mother food and a drink. As he took the money out to pay, she noticed a familiar mark on the pound coin. She looked over and saw her marking on the coin. She put on a brave face until they returned home.

When she got home, she went to the place she kept her money. After she counted her money, she realized her brother was stealing the money she was trying to save. So not only was he getting the money she owed him for her fare to London, he was also getting money from her for the rent and was stealing money from her on top of that. She was furious. That night my mother confronted him. He laughed and said, "At least I didn't steal all of it."

Shortly after that, my mother was able to move out and get her own place. I am always in awe of how she overcame so many difficulties and has still managed to thrive. My mother is so strong, and I am proud to be her son. She didn't let the trauma she has faced break her. Instead, my mother took that trauma and turned it into her trampoline. Whenever someone tried to hold her down, she bounced back even higher. No matter the obstacle she continues to come out on top. What a great example of someone who refuses to let the haters in the family hinder her hopes for a brighter and better tomorrow.

When will it end?

The saying is true: what goes around comes around. Who would have thought it would have come around so quickly? My brother Patrick went to school for plumbing and heating. Before he even attended school, he was pretty good with his hands; anything plumbing related he could do it. It was second nature to him. After finishing school, he opened Whall's

Plumbing and Heating Services. It was a small shop in a town called Peckham (in London). Though it was small, he attracted a lot of business. People all over London knew Pat.

I was pretty young at the time, but I was so proud my brother had his own business. What I didn't know was all of the underhanded things he was doing in order to keep his business going. Many people were being ripped off, bills were overdue, and the work was subpar. People began to get angry with the way my brother was handling his business. The debts continued to grow, and complaints from suppliers increased. The business was falling apart before his eyes.

I was confused. If Patrick's business was suffering, why was he driving a brand-new Range Rover and a sports car? How is it that he was able to go on international trips if he was so much in debt? I'll tell you how. He was taking out loans to keep up appearances, and when it came time to pay them back, he would go missing in action. Eventually his business closed, and the cars were repossessed. All of this took place while he remortgaged our mother's house. I believe karma came back around quicker than he expected.

Instead of doing the right thing and paying his debts, he decided to pull another scam. This time he remortgaged our sister Deborah's house. Remember, Deborah was in on the scam when they remortgaged our mother's house. Now Patrick had stooped to a new low by stealing from his sister. After Patrick got the money, he skipped town. Several months later Deborah came home to find a letter from the bank stating that her house was in the process of being foreclosed on. She didn't understand how this could have happened. In the letter they informed her she could request a hearing. When it came time to show up in court, the bank explained her husband had taken out a second mortgage that was now in default. My sister had never been married. She and Patrick have the same last name, so he was able to get away with signing the contract by himself.

Deborah was devastated. All that she and Patrick had put my mother through had come back to bite her. After the bank realized the second mortgage had been obtained via fraud, they forgave the loan. Deborah was on the verge of losing everything and would have ended up on the street. Patrick was nowhere to be found. I'm not sure if Deborah ever forgave Patrick, but their relationship was never the same. Thankfully, Deborah was able to get back on her feet. It wasn't easy, but she survived.

My mother has a phrase that I now often use: "I don't go looking for information, it always finds me." When all that transpired, Deborah told Rae all that happened with her and Patrick and how it almost sent her crazy. Of course, after Rae learned this information, she told my mother and me. I was not surprised at all with what Patrick did; however, I did feel bad for Deborah. Though I am a firm believer that what goes around comes around, no one deserves what Patrick put Deborah through.

It has been said time and time again that at the end of the day family is all you have. I would suggest family doesn't necessarily need to be blood. It could be someone who has shared in your failures and cheered you on in your triumphs. Family is supposed to be someone you can depend on, not someone you should be leery of. Sometimes you may have to distance yourself from family in order to grow. That doesn't mean you don't love them; it means you choose your peace and well-being over the drama. Losing family can be painful, but losing yourself will hurt more.

Ultimately, there is nothing wrong with being distant from your family; sometimes that is the healthy choice. But don't forget to pray for them, and in the event God blesses you with a spouse and children, teach your children to love and respect one another. The relationship I had with my siblings during my childhood was pretty good. But as I got older things became toxic. We couldn't stand each other and none of our parents tried to intervene to make it right. Yes, we were grown, but I would have at least expected them to support us in finding more constructive ways to get along. The thing is, my parents didn't have healthy relationships with their own siblings, either. So if they didn't know how to have healthy relationships with their siblings, how could they teach us?

It is too late for me to rectify relationships with my siblings because my two sisters are dead and my brother is nowhere to be found. But if you have siblings you're estranged from, I encourage you to reach out to them. Call them; try to reconcile. If you don't, you will end up like my aunts, uncles, and me, never having the option to make things better. Let us be better for our children and the children to come.

4

The Trauma of Betrayal

I Can't Believe You Would Do This to Me

I didn't have many friends growing up, especially when my mother and I moved to the U.S. Most of my friends were in London and I missed them terribly. My small group of friends in London were one of a kind. We would do everything together, from playing sports, hanging out on the weekend, and spending time at one another's houses. I recently turned forty-four and I still reminisce about those times in the mid-eighties. Sometimes I wish I could get those days back. They were indeed some wonderful times. When I think about my childhood comrades, I think how innocent we were and how I took those friendships for granted. If one of us got into trouble in school, the rest of us would cover for them. If one of us was being bullied, we would all fight; win or lose, we would be in the fight together. There was something special about Andrew, Jerome, Errol, Darren, and Franklin. They were true friends.

After being in New York for a few years it was difficult to find a group of friends I could play with on the weekends or even hang out with after school. It was exhausting trying to fit in and even more so trying to adjust to the culture. Summertime was the worst because many of the children in the city would go down south or to camp. I was pretty much a loner and kept to myself. With my mother working and my siblings three thousand miles away, I was left to my own thoughts and thirteen channels on the television.

Around the age of fourteen I joined a community choir. Every Saturday we would rehearse and have singing engagements. There were times I didn't get home until 1 a.m. My mother had a hard time believing I was in church for so long. If you ask me, I had a hard time believing it myself, and I was there.

During my time in the choir, I met some people who I thought were my friends but quickly found out they were nothing of the sort. One of them was named Sheila. We went to the same high school and sang in the choir together. Sheila introduced me to her cousin Tracy. Tracy was about two years older than I was and had a baby, but I liked her and I believed she liked me as well. After some time, we started dating.

For the first few months everything was great. Then, one day a guy named Jeffery came over to Sheila's house while Tracy and I were there. Jeffery and I didn't get along, but he was friends with Sheila, so I did my best to keep the peace. I could tell Jeffery was interested in Tracy the way he would stare at her and insert himself into our conversations. As the day went on, it started to get late, and I had to leave in order to make it home by curfew. While I was leaving, Jeffery was still there chatting with Tracy. So, before I left, I gave her a kiss and told her I would see her the following weekend. As I began walking home, Jeffery came up behind me and said he needed to talk to me. I told him to make it quick because I needed to get home. He said, "I bet you twenty dollars I can take your girl away from you." I looked him dead in the face and responded, "Tracy wouldn't want a bum like you so go ahead, give it your best shot."

The following Friday I was supposed to hang out with Tracy for the weekend. I had a dental appointment and then went to Sheila's house to meet Tracy. I was excited to see her and didn't care that my mouth was swollen and I could barely talk from the Novocain. When I arrived at Sheila's house Tracy was there and, to my surprise, so was Jeffery. I greeted everyone and went over to give Tracy a kiss. To my chagrin she turned her face and told me we needed to talk. When we walked outside Tracy told me we had to break up because she was dating someone else. I was in complete shock and at a loss for words. In that moment, Jeffery came outside and smirked, "Hey man, she made her choice."

Tracy and Jeffery went back into the house. Five minutes later, Sheila came out and asked if I was okay. I asked Sheila if she knew about Tracy and Jeffery. She said she did and that she was the one who hooked them up. So Tracy betrayed me and Sheila was the coordinator. I was so hurt all I could do was walk away. Before I could get to the end of the driveway, Jeffery came running out and asked if I had his twenty dollars. I turned around and, before I knew it, we were fighting. Sheila and her mother came and broke up the fight. Jeffery was yelling that he wanted his money. I shouted back, telling him to kiss my ass. We exchanged a few more words and I turned to walk home. Sheila caught up to me and said, "It's better this way." I looked her in the eye and told her we were no longer friends.

I was only a teenager but that began a cycle of pain, distrust, and wanting to seek revenge. I threw a wall up around my heart and felt a need to protect myself from everyone. I trusted no one; I believed no one; I started hating everyone. Some may say the way I felt about Tracy was just a childhood crush. But you can't sweep pain under the rug and minimize it as adolescence. If adolescent heartbreak is not dealt with, it can carry over into adult relationships. If we do not seek help for our childhood trauma, we may end up taking out our frustrations on our future husbands and wives. We must get a handle on our pain; it is imperative we confront our difficulties and the shame we experienced in our past. When we come face to face with the things that have restricted us from having healthy relationships and navigate the choppy waters, then and only then can we find peace.

It's time to let go. It is time to relinquish what you cannot change. I know you may have experienced trauma during your adolescent years that made you feel unworthy and useless. The fact is you are none of those things. You are better than what happened to you. You are better than those who have let you down and betrayed your heart. You are a warrior, and warriors don't give in to their frustrations, self-doubts, and hopes for a different past. Warriors stand and fight, all the time believing there is something better on the horizon. Push through the pain because there is something that is worthwhile on the other side of your pain and shame.

I take responsibility for my actions

What happened between Tracy and I snowballed into an unhealthy pattern of wanting to "get" others before they "got" me. Many of the women I dated felt my wrath. I couldn't care less if they were nice or not; I was determined to take my frustrations out on them. All of this was because I didn't know how to deal with my trauma. I didn't know what to do to free myself of the pain.

My only goal was to sleep with them a few times and be done. I wanted them to feel what I felt; I wanted them to feel the hurt, the shame, the embarrassment, the betrayal. I put my energy into sleeping with as many women as I could. My behavior never made me feel any better. It made me feel worse. I was misusing my energy and taking my pain out on innocent women—women who didn't deserve to be treated in such an awful way.

I was in so deep that it felt impossible to get out. I was lost in my trauma. I was caught up in revenge and I couldn't see a clear path out. That's the thing about vengeance: when you are blinded by seeking revenge you miss the opportunity to reflect and grow from the experience. This goes back to what I have said about sibling rivalries and family. The people you are hurting have nothing to do with the underlying issue you are struggling with. You must target the issue, not the innocent bystander.

I remember I was dating a beautiful girl named Annette. Annette was so sweet, quiet, and soft spoken. This young lady was everything I wanted in a girlfriend, but because I was so caught up in my own trauma, I ruined a great relationship. Annette and I met at a church service and there was instant attraction. Whenever we were together, I would forget about all of the trouble and trauma that surrounded me. She made me feel special. But in the back of my mind, I was still holding on to what Tracy had done to me.

Anytime I had one of those flashbacks I would take it out on Annette. If we were at the movies or watching a show at the house and there was a scene that reminded me of Tracy, I would react. My issue with Tracy had control over how I would treat Annette. I would become verbally aggressive with her. After a while, Annette couldn't take it any longer and broke up with me. I was so upset, but at the same time I needed that kick in the ass to remind me I could not and should not treat women so poorly, to remind me of how I also felt about some of the men in my life and how they treated women.

There were other women who felt my wrath as well and, for good reason, dumped me posthaste. After several failed relationships I knew it was time to take a self-inventory. I was coming close to doing the very thing that I detested. I needed to empty myself of the toxicity that was ruining relationships and destroying my mental health. The time had come for me to step back from being in a relationship and work on me. But I have trust issues, so I wasn't always comfortable sharing intimate details with anyone. I did a lot of meditating and praying. The main thing that helped me at the time and still does was reading. I've always found comfort in reading, and one of my favorite books to read was *Who Moved My Cheese?* by Spencer Johnson, M.D. I needed change in my life, and that was the perfect book for me at that time as it talks about simple ways to reduce fear and anxiety about changing. I took some of the principles from that book to help me navigate through the changes I needed. I didn't want to hem and haw any longer; I wanted to be free.

If you are serious about freeing yourself from trauma, you will have to seriously consider revisiting the urge of getting into a relationship. Just because you feel lonely doesn't mean you should get into a situation with the first person who shows interest in you. Putting yourself first and being comfortable in your own skin is necessary before you jump into a relationship. Many young people are afraid of being alone; they figure having a massive number of friends is the way to go. In all actuality, having about two or three real, genuine people in your life is all you really need. I've learned you need people around you who will not only compliment you but will also confront you when they see you slipping away from your potential. I am also aware that working on yourself is far from a waste of time. Taking the time to develop a better version of yourself is always time well spent. Letting go of things that have taken away your drive and ability is refreshing. Your mind becomes rejuvenated, your spirit refreshed, and your creative juices begin to flow. If you really want to be free, let go of the poison of bitterness in order to create space for what your heart desires. In retrospect, my former version of myself was people pleasing. I said "yes" to everything even if I didn't want to do it. Now, I have created a more mature and centered version of myself by relinquishing the things that don't offer me peace. I don't allow anyone to disturb my creativity, and most importantly, I no longer allow anyone to interrupt my self-care.

Not everyone is your friend

I can hear my mother's voice as clear as day: "Son, I don't have many friends, and you have to be careful not to call everyone your friend." My mother would drive that point home every time I would introduce someone to her as my friend. As a child I thought her words were annoying and that she didn't want me to have a social life. Growing up you always think your parents are trying to interfere with your fun. Hearing my mother say over and over again that not everyone was my friend stuck with me. Whenever I would meet someone new, my goal was to get to know them and see if they were genuine. It was important for me to see if they were worth my time and energy. Failed relationships program you to perform necessary investigations before allowing yourself to be vulnerable.

One morning I was reading an article about Prince William and how he determines who his real friends are. The article said, to the best of my recollection, that one day a student who attended the same university as Prince William asked him a question. The young man asked how he was able to trust people and know if they are his real friends? Prince William replied that it was easy. If he wanted to know if someone is a real friend, he'd tell them a fake story about his life, and if it ends up in the press he knew he couldn't trust them. But if he never heard that particular story again, he knew he could.

I of course don't condone lying, but perhaps in some cases, especially when you are concerned people are trying to take advantage of you, it can sometimes be warranted. The opportunity came for me to use that same approach. There was someone in my choir who always wanted to hang around me and offer me rides home. I didn't have a car at the time and didn't want them to think I was just using them for rides so I decided I would give our friendship a shot. Each time we had choir rehearsal this person would offer me a ride home. During our rides, we would make small talk. After a few weeks this person stepped it up a notch and started asking personal questions. I thought it quite strange that they wanted to know such private information, so I decided to try out Prince William's method. I made up a story and shared it with this individual. They were shocked at what I revealed. I was amused and suprised by my own on-the-spot creativity. After I shared this false information, they tried to dig deeper but I resisted the temptation to divulge any additional fake information. That following week when I arrived at rehearsal, a few people were whispering and looking at me strangely. I knew then my plan had worked. When rehearsal was over, I figured I would get another ride home, but this person's car was full with the same people he had been gossiping about me with. When he told me he could not give me a ride, I said that was not a problem and added, "I know you're talking negatively about me. What I told you was a lie. I was trying to figure out if you're genuine or not." I went on to say, "You proved my point, and you and I are no longer friends." This individual was taken aback.

After that incident, I started to keep more to myself and didn't allow anyone to get close. My mother's words about everyone not being my friend proved to be true. I didn't allow this realization to ruin my entire perspective on humankind. I just knew I would have to be cautious about those I let into my life.

I let my guard down

Actions speak louder than words. Also, when people consistently say the right things, it can sometimes lead you to ignore their actions. But ultimately, actions can cause trauma, trauma that will affect the way you deal with people. When you are caught up with the excitement of a new romantic relationship, it can suffocate one of your most valuable senses: discernment. You may overlook your ability to detect when something is wrong or right when you get distracted by someone else's charisma. The headiness of sensual words can cloud your judgment and paralyze your perception. Therefore, it is so important not to get involved in a relationship when you are vulnerable. When you're vulnerable, your emotions are unstable, and you have likely not completely healed from the last relationship you were in. Just because you have dismissed a traumatic situation from your mind doesn't mean you have healed from the experience.

Taking time to heal is necessary for your spiritual, mental, and physical growth. Any medical doctor will tell you after a traumatic injury or surgery it is imperative that you heal. If you do not take time to heal, you risk causing more damage to the area of concern. You set yourself back because you didn't take the necessary steps to fully complete your healing process. Trying to get back out there too soon is unhealthy and nothing good can come from a rushed relationship. Just because something may look good on the outside doesn't mean it is good for you.

I must admit I was one of those people who would jump from one relationship to another out of fear of being by myself. I would settle for who would give me attention instead of being selective about who would enhance my life, and vice versa. That's how I ended up with Patricia. Patricia had caramel skin and an outstanding body. She was incredibly beautiful. Her personality on the surface seemed to match mine. She was driven to achieve her dreams and accomplish her goals.

One evening Patricia and I attended a party at a mutual friend's house where we spent the time flirting and talking about life. On the surface, things felt good, but I wanted to get to know her on a deeper level. As the party was winding down, I walked her to her car and asked if I could see her again. We exchanged numbers and began dating. Everything happened so quickly. Before I knew it, we were in a relationship and having sex. No matter what kind of date we were on, the night always ended in sex. That was our relationship: hang out, then sex. After a while we both agreed we should slow down and get to know one another.

I began to let my guard down. We started to share things with one another and talk about the future. I started thinking she could be the one. One day I brought her home to meet my mother. I was nervous about what my mother would think. When Patricia and my mother met it seemed like they were getting along. The evening ended and Patricia left. As soon as I closed the door, my mother looked at me square in the face and said, "What do you see in her?" I didn't know what she meant and, truthfully speaking, I couldn't answer the question. I didn't answer my mother's question because I had nothing of value to say, which was concerning to me, perhaps because she was right.

One night before I went to bed, I got down on my knees and asked God if Patricia was the one for me. That night I had a dream that Patricia was cheating on me with another man. I tried to make out who the man was but couldn't.

The next day I had no appetite and felt on edge. Patricia and I barely spoke that day but ended up seeing each other at church that night. Normally we would embrace with a hug, but that night she was cold and distant. Just before choir rehearsal was about to start, I went looking for Patricia but couldn't find her. Her car was outside, but she was nowhere to be found. I called her phone, but no answer. I called again and her phone went straight to voicemail. I was looking all around the church but saw no sign of Patricia. I stopped outside the door of one of the offices and tried calling her again. I heard her phone ring and then abruptly go to voicemail. I was getting irritated. Several minutes later Patricia finally came out of the office. She was stunned to see me standing there. After a moment of silence, she yelled out, "Don't start with me!" I asked her what she had been doing in the office and who she was with. She ignored me so I grabbed her by her arms and asked her again. She pulled away from me, so I headed back to the office where I had found her. To my surprise, it was our mutual friend—the friend who had hosted the party where we first officially met. The friend tried to play things off like nothing was wrong.

I knew I needed to get out of there before I ended up doing something I would regret. My dream was right. I was just in disbelief that this man I called a friend would betray me the way he had. The moment I let my guard down, I got sucker punched, not just by Patricia but by someone I'd known for quite some time.

I was traumatized and heartbroken. I fell into a deep depression. I couldn't eat, sleep, or focus at work or church. I even contemplated suicide. One morning I was at the bus stop and I started to step off the sidewalk into moving traffic. That's how low I was. The truth is I am too much of a coward to take my own life and something inside of me said it wasn't worth it. I didn't understand how this could happen to me. I had tried to be a good man and it seemed like the more I tried, the more I failed.

I tried to call Patricia to get some clarity. After several attempts at reaching out she finally called me back. She told me it would be best if we just broke up because she was moving to another state. Before I could get a word in, she hung up the phone. For several months I kept asking myself what I could have done to be a better boyfriend. I started to blame myself for everything. I spent days in bed and refused to talk to anyone. I completely shut down.

Then one day a colleague came by my house and told me to stop sleeping my life away and that things would get better. He had no idea what was going on with me, but his words were what I needed to hear. I got up, showered, went to the barbershop, and had lunch with that same colleague. To this day he has no idea the impact he had on me. Sometimes all it takes is someone coming into your life and reminding you your life is worth living. You may hit some bumps in the road. You may have to start over a few more times. But when it's all said and done, things will get better. It is so important you believe things will get better and think about the people you're with and whether they help you believe that. Otherwise, you will likely continue to stay in the rut you are in. When you finally open the shades and allow the light to shine in, you will realize your worth and recognize you are better than your current circumstances.

After some time, I got over Patricia. It wasn't easy. But I decided to forgive her and our mutual friend. To be completely honest it took me years to get over what our mutual friend did to me. I even left the church we were attending because I couldn't stand the sight of him. I needed to get away before I lost all control. Every day I had to let go of the pain and remember this happened for a reason and that I would overcome this difficult season of my life.

When I completely let go of that traumatic experience, I was eventually able to see my former friend face to face. I even gave him a hug and asked him how everything was going in his life. Let me tell you, that is growth for me. At one time in my life, and I'm ashamed of this, I would have beat him until my fist got tired, or came close. But that would have only proven I wasn't fully over the incident and was too immature to control my emotions.

When you can see someone who has wronged you and still act with grace, you know you have finally been liberated from the pain. It is my hope that whenever you meet the person who has betrayed you, you will display grace and kindness. Don't give energy to the past. Use your energy to create an atmosphere of tranquility and joy. Don't let what you've gone through define you. You are bigger, better, and much wiser than that. You should be proud of the new and improved you!

5

The Trauma of Church

I'm Tired of This Church

There is a YouTube video that went viral on social media of a six-year-old boy who said, "I am tired of this church." There have been sermons preached based on that video. Comedians have had a field day making jokes about the young boy's candidness regarding his feelings toward the church. To be brutally honest, the young man said what most of us are afraid to say. Many of us would be too fearful that our parents, the pastor, or even God would chastise us for feeling the way he feels. After all, the church is God's house and we shouldn't be tired of God's house, right? Well, it's not the building that is the issue, it is the people who occupy the building.

I have been "saved" (accepted Jesus Christ as my personal savior) since the age of seventeen. I have been an ordained minister for twenty-one years. I've been involved in ministry for thirty years. I have served as a youth choir president, praise-and-worship leader, youth minister, associate minister, senior pastor, and interim pastor. If I know nothing else, I know church and I know church people.

What I didn't know is that church people are some of the most ruthless, conniving, underhanded, deceitful, and hypocritical people you could meet. Let me be clear. I am not referring to Christians. I am referring to people who use their free time to wreak havoc in an organization that was designed to express love for Jesus Christ. There is a major difference between Christians and church people. Christians know that if it had not been for the blood of Jesus Christ shed on Calvary's cross, they would be lost. Church people act like they are the ones who died for humanity and that their blood will wipe your sins away. Church people will justify their nastiness toward another individual by saying, "God is still working on me." That's what Dietrich Bonhoeffer would call "cheap grace." Christians will acknowledge their wrong and seek the ministry of reconciliation; that is costly grace. The issue is the organization called the church is filled with too many people in leadership who operate in cheap grace and not enough of those who move in costly grace.

As I stated, I have been in the church for a long time, and I have witnessed many things that would cause the average Joe to never step foot in a church again. I have come face to face with some of the most disrespectful people who call themselves pastors, deacons, trustees, evangelists, bishops, and so on. There have been moments I almost came to blows with people. That is not what church is supposed to be. It is supposed to be a place of restoration, refuge, cultivation, peace, and tranquility.

The problem is church has turned into a political and social club. I feel like going to church in this generation is more like going to the slots in Vegas. Sometimes you hit it big where the pastor and people do their absolute best to express the love of Jesus, and others are snake eyes on the craps table. They'll cut you too short to shit. I have experienced both ends of the spectrum, and the snake eyes side has traumatized me.

Sing unto the Lord a new song

As I mentioned, I joined a community choir in New York at the age of fourteen. I never really went to church that much in London and if I did it was only Sunday school. So, joining the choir and traveling to different churches was a culture shock to me. People would jump up and shout or claim to be filled with the Holy Spirit. Some would be speaking in a weird language claiming it would be tongues. What I couldn't figure out was how they were so passionate about speaking to God in another language but couldn't speak to one another in English. There would be people who said they had the gift of prophecy and could tell what would happen in the future.

So many things would go on in these churches where the choir would sing. As a child I thought it all to be a joke. As I got older, I understood there are people who would play with God, and then you had those who were serious about their commitment to God. In my observation, it was very hard to decipher who was genuine and who was artificial. As I matured in God, it became much easier to tell the difference. While singing with the choir I learned how to sing about Jesus but never really understood who Jesus is.

One day as the choir was riding in the van heading to a singing engagement, I asked a question about church to one of the ministers who played the organ. It escapes me now what the question was; all I know is it was concerning Jesus. As the minister was about to answer my question, the driver of the van interrupted abruptly and said to me, "Your stupid ass doesn't know?" I was shocked. I asked the driver who he was and why he was inserting himself in my conversation. He responded, "I'm a minister, and you must be a stupid mother-fucker." Again, I was blown away by this man and his use of such language. What was even more shocking is that he claimed to be a minister. I told him I didn't know ministers talked like that. He yelled back, "Don't you worry about what the fuck I say, little bitch." Meanwhile the choir was laughing hysterically about the interaction between me and the driver. Even the minister I had originally directed the question to was laughing uncontrollably. I didn't understand how they could call themselves Christians but act in such a hateful way. Unfortunately, that was one of the first of many disappointing interactions with Christianity.

I thought about leaving the choir after that but because I was always home by myself and my siblings were three thousand miles away, I decided to stick it out. Therein lies the problem: we are afraid to remove ourselves from toxic environments out of fear of being alone. Being part of the choir felt like an opportunity to fill a void of loneliness. Honestly, though, it was never filled; even when I was around those forty-plus choir members, I was still alone. Unless we had to sing at a church event, I never really saw the other choir members, even though I went to school with some of them. Don't get me wrong; I had some good times in the choir. I was able to make a few friends and learn some things when I became president of the youth choir at my church. All in all, I had my ups and downs, and I was able to make it through.

As all of us in the choir got older, some started to leave because they were heading off to college and/or becoming ministers in their churches. I, on the other hand, was trying to find myself and somewhat trying to fit into something I had already grown out of. About a year before I left the choir, I agreed to be the assistant business manager. The volunteer job involved calling choir members and reminding them of rehearsals every week, accepting or declining singing engagements based on our schedule, and helping to collect monthly dues. I was excited to be involved. I even went a step further and planned our concerts and one of the anniversaries. I gave it my all.

During the end of that year the business manager stepped down from his position to pursue other things. I just knew I was going to be asked to take over. At the last concert I put together, the president of the choir announced that the business manager was leaving. He went on to say we had a replacement for the position. My stomach turned and I felt a rush of excitement because I just knew he was about to announce me as the new business manager. Hell, I was doing all the work, so it was only right it would be me. To my chagrin, though, it was not me. My heart sank. The president went on to say, "We thank Tristram for his hard work, but we feel it best to hand it over to someone more mature." I was so embarrassed. How was I mature enough to make all the calls, schedule engagements, and plan concerts but not enough to hold the position? I was pissed beyond measure. In one of the rehearsals the president even had the nerve to say in front of everyone that he never intended to make me the business manager. I felt used and abused. About a month after that I decided to leave the choir.

What I experienced was the beginning of an unhealthy trend of rejection and feeling worthless. When people try to make you feel like you are not good enough it can affect your productivity and suffocate your potential. The people who make you feel that way are not qualified to speak on what you can or cannot do. You have to believe in who you are.

Leaving the choir was the best decision I could have made. I needed a fresh start, and I was looking for more to do. Singing in the choir was an interesting experience, but I wasn't fulfilled. Looking back at that time in my life I am pleased with what I learned. The life lessons I experienced in that ministry served as a foundation for where I was about to go. Everything I went through in the choir was preparing me for something, I just didn't know what. What I did know is I needed to experience something different, something more structured. I wanted to grow in Christianity, and I felt the only way to do that was to search for a new church home.

There's no place like Mount Zion

While I was in the community choir we would sing every year for the birthday celebration of Dr. J. B. Smith, pastor of Mount Zion Baptist Church. The church would be jam-packed with choirs from all over the tristate area. If you didn't get there an hour before the service started, you wouldn't get a seat. Dr. Smith's birthday service was probably one of my favorite engagements. Dr. Smith was also a singer, so after all the choirs had given their musical selections, he would also sing a few songs to close us out.

After several years of attending Dr. Smith's musical, I decided to hear him preach. I found out he was speaking at a Dr. Martin Luther King birthday service. I decided to check it out. The service was quite long and so was Dr. Smith's sermon. But I was in awe of what he presented that Monday evening. I made up my mind I was going to his church on Sunday. That Sunday morning, I arrived at Mount Zion early just in case I couldn't get a seat. Fortunately for me, not many people attended the Sunday school before the main service, so I was able to get a seat. The Sunday service was filled with litanies, responsive readings, ceremonial prayers, and so many other things that caused the service to be three hours long. Two hours into the service, Dr. Smith finally delivered his sermon. His topic was "Heaven or Hell? You Choose." It turned out he talked about hell so much that I wanted no part of it and decided to rededicate my life to the Lord and join the church. It was January 1996. I was pleased with my decision, and I felt this was the right decision for me.

While being a member of Mount Zion I joined the youth choir and became one of Dr. Smith's assistants. I was really getting into the groove of things. I was very happy. Several weeks later my mother joined, and we were both baptized on Holy Thursday. Things seemed to be moving in the right direction. I had a church with a wonderful pastor and a congregation that embraced me and my mother. Two years later, on June 26, 1998, my beloved pastor went home to be with the Lord. I was so sad. The man who baptized and fed me the Word of God was gone. I felt lost, upset, and disappointed I didn't get more time. I was mad with God. I finally found a place where I felt like I belonged, and now the pastor was dead. It took me a long time to get over Dr. Smith's death. He had made me feel special, like I could do anything. He had a way with words, and he practiced what he preached. I was proud to call Dr. Smith my pastor.

A week later we had a three-day celebration for Dr. Smith. A musical, a traditional homegoing service, and then the graveside service. Once the graveside service was over the graveyard workers lifted the casket to Dr. Smith's slot in the mausoleum. It felt like they slammed his casket into that cold, brick hole. The cries of his family and parishioners filled the air. There was not a dry eye in the mausoleum section of the cemetery. And then that was it. The services were over, and we left the remains of Dr. J. B. Smith at his final resting place.

Church wasn't the same without Dr. Smith. The summer season felt like winter, and every Sunday for four months Dr. Smith's seat was draped with his robe. Many of the parishioners had known him for the forty-plus years he had been pastor and had a hard time moving on. I hadn't known him long, but the few years I did know him were impactful, and I will never forget them.

Several months later Dr. Smith's son, Reverend Damien Smith, moved into the role as senior pastor of Mount Zion. He had a different approach to pastoring than his father. It was a hard adjustment. Reverend Smith was not as compassionate as his father. Maybe it was because he was in the armed forces, so he had a completely different mindset. Reverend Smith gave orders; his father asked for help.

It wasn't long after Reverend Smith became pastor that we had our own run-in. One day Reverend Smith said something to me in a very condescending tone, and I pushed back by saying, "I don't know who you are talking to." Our early interactions were tense but eventually things smoothed out. For a while it worked out.

In 1997, after only being at the church for about a year I was elected as president of the youth choir. The truth is I wasn't even vying for this position. Initially my friend Mark was the president, but he did a lousy job. When it came time for our choir anniversary, Mark didn't invite any choirs or organize a celebration. So, because I had contacts from my years of being the assistant business manager for the community choir, I leaped into action and called in some favors. Our anniversary was saved, but the choir was angry about Mark's inaction. So, when election time came around, the choir voted me in. Remember, Mark was the one who was hitting Michelle. I could tell he was jealous I took his position because he no longer had any input to give or ideas to share.

After I was elected president, I went to work. We started having youth revivals, workshops, concerts, and anniversaries. The concerts were so successful, choirs that weren't invited came anyway in hopes to get on the program. I have to say, God really used me to bring a new level of excitement back into the choir. We also had bowling and skating parties, car washes, and barbecues. I even instituted an annual Back 2 School Extravaganza. I was proud of all the hard work we were doing.

I quickly learned, though, that not everyone who smiles in your face and gives you a compliment wishes you well. There was a woman at Mount Zion named Mary Carter. She directed the children's choir (ages three to twelve). The youth choir was my area (ages thirteen to twenty-five). Sister Carter didn't have many children in her choir but Reverend Smith allowed her to continue with them. She was faithful and he didn't want to discourage her efforts or discourage the little children. You could tell Sister Carter wanted to be more involved with the youth. On many occasions she tried to insert herself in our meetings but wasn't successful in her attempts. When people are desperate for attention, they will do what it takes to take down anyone who stands in their way. As the youth choir was growing, I was also dealing with my call to the ministry. My pastor recognized the call and began to prepare me for this new role in my life. When Reverend Smith announced my call to the congregation, I got a standing ovation, except for Mark and Sister Carter. I knew then that I needed to watch my back. When a person is jealous of you, they turn into an unrecognizable person. The funny thing is that all of what I was doing in the church, I never asked for—it just fell into my lap.

On January 30, 2000, I gave my initial sermon and was licensed to preach. In a predominately Black church, when someone is called to preach, they go through a time of training. It could be one to three years of learning from your pastor and applying to school to see if this is really what you believe God is calling you to do. After that time period the pastor will schedule a date for when you will present your first sermon. Depending on how well you do, you are presented with a license to preach and teach in your local church. At that point you are not an ordained minister; you are in training to one day be ordained.

It was an exciting time in my life. The youth department continued to grow, and I started a boys and girls mentoring program. We had field trips and invited guest speakers to come talk about the benefits of being a good mentor. I was very happy with the way my life was going. Remember, as you are excited about how God is raising you up, there are people who can't see that and might even be plotting your demise. You have to stay prayerful and committed.

As my ministry and popularity were growing among the young people, the church, and community, a nasty lie was being spread about me. Sister Carter would tell the parents of the children that they needed to be careful with me around their children because I might try to have sex with their sons. She also told them she didn't think it was healthy I still presided over the youth department at the age of twenty-three. The rumors started to spread, people in the congregation started to treat me funny, and complaints were made to the pastor. I was crushed. To add insult to injury, my pastor believed the rumors and removed me from the youth department. I couldn't believe these people I had ministered to believed I was a pedophile. What was also devastating was that people who I thought were my friends were spreading rumors that I was gay.

I fell into a deep depression. After about a week or so I confronted my pastor, but he insisted folks wouldn't just make this stuff up. I asked him if he believed I had touched any young people and, if so, what proof he had. He told me to go home and said we would talk about things later. As I was leaving the church, the nephew of Sister Carter called me a "faggot." I turned around and beat his ass right in between the office of the pastor and the sanctuary. I can't remember who broke up the altercation; all I remember is I lost control. After I calmed down, I went home. Reverend Smith called and said he heard what happened and that I couldn't go around fighting people in the church. I told him he should have defended me and that I was disappointed in him and the church. He said, "Well, you can leave." I told him to "go to hell" and hung up the phone. He called back and told me I was officially removed from the pulpit. I responded with, "Fuck you and your pulpit" and hung up.

That Sunday night I cried all night long into the morning. I couldn't believe all my hard work had ended abruptly. I was traumatized. I was disgusted that people would make up such vicious lies about me. I left Mount Zion broken and unsure of what would happen next. Pastors in the area cancelled engagements and I was blackballed from our Baptist association. I was a complete wreck. So many things were going through my mind and I wasn't sure what would come of my ministry. My heart was shattered.

About a year later I went back to Mount Zion, but it wasn't the same. In 2007 I left completely, hoping and praying God had something better in mind. I never did get an apology from the pastor, Sister Carter, her nephew, or those who helped spread the rumors. Sometimes you won't get an apology; you have to move on knowing the ones who hurt you will have to face the consequences of their decisions. Your job is to learn from the lessons and use what has happened as fuel for the next level of your life.

This can't be church

On Friday, October 3, 2014, I was called to be the senior pastor of Haven Baptist Church in Haven, Connecticut. I was beyond excited to finally get my opportunity to lead God's people. I'd had the opportunity to preach for Haven Baptist on several

THE TRAUMA OF CHURCH

occasions. One Sunday afternoon, after I had preached for their Black history program, one of the deacons approached me about applying. I figured it was a God moment because I told God that in order for me to apply to this church, they would need to ask me—that's how I would know if it was of God or not. I agreed to apply. After eight months, the church extended me the offer to be their next pastor and I gladly accepted. I believed this was my time to do ministry.

That weekend I prepared my sermon and asked God to help me with this new assignment. That Sunday morning, I was excited and nervous; all I wanted to do was please God and serve his people with integrity. I arrived at the church that Sunday morning around 9 a.m. When I pulled into my parking spot, I noticed the parking lot was completely empty and the church doors were locked. I wondered where everyone was. Sunday school started in half an hour and no one was there. I got back into my car and I waited. At 9:25 a.m. the church secretary, who happened to be the Sunday school superintendent, finally showed up. She asked me what I was doing there so early. She said people typically started strolling in around 9:45 a.m. and the deacons are never on time anyway.

I wondered what the hell I had gotten myself into. I finally walked into the church and headed to my office. Of course, that door was locked, and because it was my first day, I didn't have a key. About an hour later one of the deacons showed up with the key to let me in. I settled down and got myself ready for my first service as the pastor. Fifteen minutes before service started my wife, Kimberlee, called me to help her with the kids. I headed out the side door toward the car and noticed one of the members walking up the front stairs. I told her good morning, but she looked at me with pure hatred, rolled her eyes, and stomped up the stairs. I didn't know her so I didn't understand her response. I let it go and headed toward my family. I helped my wife inside and headed back to my office.

Eleven o'clock rolled around and I heard nothing, no organ, no keyboard, and no drums. All I heard was people talking. I went upstairs and Deacon Stan was having a casual conversation with one of the parishioners. It was now after 11 a.m. I told Deacon Stan we should get the service started. I headed back downstairs to get my Bible and iPad. As the ushers escorted me in, I noticed the same woman who gave me the nasty look was on the praise team. Her name is Celina Saunders. I couldn't believe someone with such a nasty disposition had the nerve to be on the mic encouraging people to praise God but refusing to speak to the pastor.

I took my seat and the service went on and more people arrived. When it was time to give my remarks, most of the congregation was full of smiles except for Celina and her sister Martha. I know this because they were on the second pew. Why is it all the nasty, mean, and disrespectful church folk sit up front? In my remarks I shared how I was looking forward to working with the board and serving the entire congregation. After my remarks I was met with claps and cheers. It seemed the church was ready for a new beginning.

For several weeks things seemed to be moving along. People were joining and I believed God was pleased with the progress. The only thing was I wanted to know what the issue was with Celina. It was my desire to work with everyone, so I called a meeting with the chairman of deacons and Celina to find out what issues there might be and to discuss them openly.

Celina sent word through the secretary that she would be bringing her sister Martha and her nephew Larry. The meeting was scheduled for Monday evening at the church.

The atmosphere was very tense. Celina was looking meaner than ever and her sister Martha looked like she'd been sucking on lemons all day. I opened with prayer and shared my concerns. While I was talking, Celina never took her eyes off me. If looks could kill I would be dead right now. Once I finished, Celina began to go off in a wild rant. She began by saying she didn't agree with me being the pastor and she couldn't understand why her other sister, Reverend Stern, would always invite me to preach. Her sister Reverend Stern was the interim pastor before I came on board. As Celina was ranting, I zoned out for about ten seconds and wondered how many damn sisters she had in this church. I quickly zoned back in to make sure I didn't miss any of the bullshit that was coming out of her mouth. Celina was saying she didn't think I could preach and didn't agree with what I said from the pulpit. At that point I had had enough. After she brought her venomous remarks to an end, I kindly reminded her I was the pastor and I hoped we would be able to work together. I closed out the meeting with prayer and asked the chairman of deacons, Deacon Bond, to stay behind for a moment so we could talk.

I was furious. I asked him why he hadn't said anything. All he said was I had to be patient with Celina and that this would blow over. But I knew this wasn't about to blow over, it was about to blow up. The thing that bothered me the most was I felt no one in the room had my back; no one present felt Celina's behavior was inappropriate. I later found out that the Saunders family held the majority of leadership positions in the church. They were on the deacon board, trustee board, choir, musician staff, praise team, and ushers, just to name a few. Once I found out the majority of the church was part of the Saunders family, I knew nothing good could come of this. I wondered again what the hell I had gotten myself into. The Saunders family was known for causing trouble in the church and gave the last two pastors a very difficult time. They would be very disrespectful in meetings and didn't care who they stepped on to get a position in the church. Several members told me I had to watch out for the Saunders family because they would stick together even when they knew one of their family members was wrong. People told me they would come after me with everything they had. I figured I better stay in prayer and be ready at all times.

As time went on, the church grew and people started joining and others left because more of the Saunders family started coming back. Word on the street was this new pastor didn't take any shit. Don't get me wrong; I wasn't a bully, but I wanted to show the church I was there to work with everyone, not just certain people. When we had church meetings, they didn't linger on for hours; we were in and out within forty-five minutes. We had an agenda and we stuck to it, and that was that. You could tell when we had church meetings that the Saunders family was up to no good because they all sat together staring me down. They tried to derail a few meetings but I made sure we stuck to the agenda.

Things started to look up for the church and my ministry until one of the Saunders family members accused me of sleeping with her cousin. One night as I was driving home from Bible study, Reverend Henderson called. She said there was something important we needed to discuss. She went on to say she didn't have Facebook but there was a picture going around on Facebook with my arm around Sister Terri, and her cousin Tasha said that that looked inappropriate. She described the picture to me over the phone. I interrupted and asked if this was the picture we took at my pastoral installation service. She said it was. I went on to tell Reverend Henderson that the picture was not just of me and Terri but the entire pastoral installation committee and that my wife was at my side along with the rest of the committee members. Reverend Henderson interrupted and said Tasha was telling everyone the picture didn't look right and that people were beginning to talk.

I was heated. The moment things had started to turn in a positive direction, here came someone trying to desecrate the ministry and poison the integrity of my leadership. After I hung up with Reverend Henderson, I told my wife the story. She was also upset. The next few days I couldn't sleep. My reputation was on the line all because of this damn family that had it out for me from the beginning. That Friday we had a church meeting; afterward I called a meeting with the deacons and Terri. I explained what happened and that the situation needed to be handled expeditiously. I informed the deacons I wanted Terri, her husband, Tasha, the deacons, and my wife to meet after church on Sunday. I needed to defuse this bomb before it destroyed my ministry and the integrity of the church.

Sunday came and I think that was the shortest sermon I have ever preached in my life. It was important I extinguish this fire. We all sat in the office. I did not open with prayer; I got straight to the point. I asked Tasha what she was thinking by accusing me of trying to sleep with her cousin—a terrible rumor that could've destroyed two marriages. Tasha sat there for a moment and then said she was just looking out for her cousin because she was concerned about her. I jumped right back in and asked why she didn't just call her cousin, or the deacons, for that matter, if she was so concerned. At this point I was beyond pissed. I wanted to slap the shit out of her for all the trouble she was trying to stir up. I said, "Thank God my wife knows that I am not that dude and Terri's husband knows she is not that type of woman. You should be ashamed of yourself." After I had calmed down, the deacons came to my defense. That was the first and only time that happened.

One of the deacons closed out in prayer and Tasha ran out of there like her ass was on fire. I never saw her again. It took me a long time to get over that situation because it wasn't only Tasha who was involved. It was some of her aunts and even Terri's mother who had a hand in trying to spread this rumor. How disgusting can you be that you would sacrifice your own daughter's integrity just to take down the pastor? I had to pull myself together. I couldn't allow them to pull me down to their level. I had thoughts about suing Tasha for defamation of character, but I left her in God's hands.

The trauma of that incident kept me on edge for a while. I trusted no one in that church, especially those with the last name Saunders. I was always on high alert, which was exhausting. I finally prayed long and hard about it and God liberated me from it. There is a passage of scripture that helped me during that difficult time. The scripture is Jeremiah 12:5: "If you have raced with men on foot, and they have wearied you, how will you compete with horses? And if in a safe land you are so trusting, what will you do in the thicket of the Jordan?" (ESV).

This scripture helped me realize God was preparing me for something greater than where I was. I had to have tough skin to survive ministry.

Ministry is not for the weakhearted; it is for those who will endure to the end. God will give you the courage you need to face adversity. God will use certain situations to remind you that you have been built for this, and there is nothing anyone can do to stop God's plan for your life. As traumatic as that situation was for me and my family, we survived because of our endurance and willingness to keep fighting until God took us out of the fight.

Here we go again

By nature, I am a very private person. What people know about me is what I want them to know. I've been that way for a long time because in my teens and early twenties I would share things because I thought people were genuine. The truth is those people just wanted to get close enough to me to find out information to report back to people who took issue with me. When I finally got wise to the game, I made up in my mind that people would only get as close as I allowed them to.

Haven Baptist really started to grow. In fact, we were discussing the possibility of adding another service, that's how well the church was doing. Members were inviting their coworkers, family, and friends to our service and I was grateful for what the Lord was doing. The word was out about Haven Baptist Church.

One of the deacons, Deacon Stan, was working with a woman I went to high school with. One day, while at work, Deacon Stan invited her to church. She asked him who the pastor was and he told her my name. She told him she had gone to school with me. Deacon Stan took that as an opportunity to try to gather information about me. He asked her how I was in school. She said I had been very quiet and kept to myself but, all in all, seemed to be a good dude. Deacon Stan dug a little deeper. He asked who I hung out with, indicating, "We don't want no faggot pastor." She laughed this comment off and said all she knew was that I kept to myself.

During a deacons' meeting, Deacon Stan shared with me that he worked with someone I went to school with. He showed me a picture of her on Facebook, and I said I remembered her. Deacon Stan told me he had invited her to church. A few weeks later I received a Facebook message from the woman sharing with me how she worked with Deacon Stan and planned to come to the church. She went on to say that, unfortunately, she wasn't comfortable coming to the church because when she was speaking with our deacon he tried to find out if I was gay because he didn't want a "faggot" for a pastor. I thanked her for her honesty and wished her well.

Again, here was someone who was supposed to watch my back and help build the church of God but instead was digging for shit that was not there. Unfortunately, in some churches you have people who are obsessed with gossip and slander. And if that person has issues with you and your leadership, where their position is threatened, then they will do everything in their power to tear you down. I had flashbacks of Mary Carter from Mount Zion Baptist. I was absolutely infuriated with Deacon Stan. The next time I saw Deacon Stan, I confronted him in front of the rest of the deacons. I shared with the deacons what the young lady shared with me. Deacon Stan was in shock and the rest of the deacons were embarrassed. I must admit I lost my cool. I told him, "You are supposed to be a deacon, but instead you are gossiping and starting rumors about your pastor." Then I just lost it. I said to him, "If I'm not fucking one of your sons, don't worry about who the hell I'm fucking." I walked out and went home.

The trauma I encountered at Haven Baptist was gut wrenching. Every time I turned around there was always something brewing to destroy my character. There was always someone from that damn Saunders family who thought they could disrespect me and I should just sit there and take it. Some churches have members who are more concerned with how much control they can gain in church. Many of them have no control at their jobs or in their homes. So, if they get a leadership role in church, it goes straight to their heads. Many of them have ruined good solid churches and have caused pastors to be so frustrated that they quit and even sue the church because of them. I had enough of the bullshit. I was mentally exhausted, and it was taking a major toll on my wife and kids.

I prayed hard and I prayed long. I finally felt a release to resign from Haven Baptist. It was the best decision I could have ever made concerning my ministry. My wife was overjoyed, and my children were delighted they didn't have to go back to that church. For the first time in over four years, I slept through the night. Once I left Haven Baptist, I did some traveling and spent a lot of time with my wife and children. It was the rest that I needed. If I hadn't resigned from Haven Baptist my mental health would have deteriorated. I believe I would have had a nervous breakdown. I needed to do what was best for me.

There will be some people who will tell you to stick it out through toxic situations. That's all good for people who have not been through what you have been through. You must take care of your mental health. You are not obligated to suffer through traumatic events. Recognize what is happening is unhealthy for you and remove yourself from anyone or anything that threatens your peace. Then pursue the opposite. Choose happiness, tranquility, stability—and choose you. I don't care if you are a pastor, teacher, garbage man, janitor, or the cashier at McDonald's. Your mental health is important for you and for your family. When you feel overwhelmed, pray, see a therapist, but don't let your mental health go unserved. You are valuable; you are worth investing in your own peace of mind. The trauma I have gone through in church almost caused me not to go back. I started to really hate church and despise the people who attended. Thankfully, it is my relationship with God that has sustained me.

I was in a real dark place the last two and a half years at Haven Baptist. I started drinking heavily and started to smoke marijuana again. I used those things to cope with the pressures of being a pastor. I didn't want to be the pastor anymore. I couldn't trust the deacons, I couldn't trust the trustees, and I sure as hell couldn't trust the ministers because they were vying for my position. It was so bad I couldn't even trust some of the other pastors in the area because they were hoping to apply for the role of senior pastor as soon as I left. All I could do was pray, and when I thought God wasn't listening, I turned to drinking and smoking. I started having panic attacks and only getting about four hours of sleep a night. It was a truly dark time. The reason I stayed so long is because I didn't want to disappoint

God. I didn't want to disappoint the people who appreciated my ministry and the people who were truly praying for me. Then I realized it's okay to walk away from an assignment that has run its course. I felt a burden lift off my shoulders.

Two weeks before I resigned, I called a church meeting and shared with the congregation my concerns. Needless to say, not many folks were pleased with my comments. After I explained my point of view, I asked them to pray with me as we sought guidance from the Lord. Then I closed out in prayer. Two days later, Deacon Bond, who was the chairman of deacons, called and said three-fourths of the church called him and was requesting a meeting with me. I said that three-fourths of the church didn't want to meet with me, and that it was that damn Saunders family that had called him and that he didn't have a backbone to tell them no. I went on further to say that I would not attend any meeting with them and hung up the phone. Deacon Bond scheduled the meeting on Bible study night and as chairman of the deacons, made the announcement in church without my permission. After the announcement, I informed the congregation that I would not be attending any such frivolous meeting and that I would be at the church that day to teach Bible study, not to attend a ridiculous meeting. Two weeks later I was at the church for Bible study and the congregation was downstairs waiting for me. No one attended the Bible study, so I went home.

Later that night, Deacon Bond called me and left a muffled message. I didn't want to call him back, but I did. He informed me I was removed from the pulpit for two weeks and that I would need to meet with the congregation before returning. I responded and said, "Are all the deacons present?" He said yes.

I asked if I was on speaker phone, and he said yes. I said, "Consider this my official resignation, effective immediately, and you, Deacon Bond, can go straight to hell," and I hung up.

I resigned Wednesday, June 26, 2019, at 9 p.m. Sometimes I think about what I could have done better. Then I realize there was nothing I could have done, because it was all part of God's plan for my life. That night I slept like a baby for eight hours straight; my wife had to wake me up because I slept so long. It was just what I needed. Currently I'm not pastoring any local church, and I am at peace with that decision. I'm not sure if God will lead me in that direction again. Either way, I am content with what I learned and what I accomplished. I made it through that dark season by trusting God and his plan for me. I want to encourage you to find the light in your darkness, and that light will guide you to your next season.

6
The Trauma of Job Loss
All You Are Is Hired Help

We have been programmed to go to school, study, graduate with high honors, get a job, work for about forty years, and retire with a gold watch and a sizable pension. That is what society calls success. Society has created this limited definition of success, suggesting if you fail to achieve that definition, you are doomed. If you dare to resist what your society, or even your family and friends, expect you to do you are considered an outcast, a misfit, or a rebel without a cause. So what do many of us do? We succumb to the words of those who don't have to wake up each day with our regrets weighing on their minds. Often people who are invested in dictating what your life should be are unaware of where their lives are heading. Instead of worrying about what others want for our journey, we should be pursuing our own goals, not the goals of others.

After we have locked down a job or a job locks us down, we become bound by the rules of another system that tells us to be creative but ultimately stifles our creativity. Now we're stuck in a rut, in a vicious cycle of doing the same thing over and over again. We have become experts in going in circles and fearing disrupting the status quo. So, instead of being who we were created to be, we become someone else's creation.

When that happens, your ideas no longer feel valid, your creative flow comes to a standstill, you become stale. The authentic you goes through an unwanted transformation, and before you know it, you don't even recognize yourself. There is trauma that comes with being bullied into a version of someone else's idea of you. Discovering who you are is always a battle within yourself. Once you have achieved that, you must also battle with the system that tried to prevent you from your discovery. Neither of these are easy battles, but if you focus on the person you know you can be, you can prevail.

When you're struggling with feeling pressured to become someone else's version of you, it is important to see how you got to that point. How you ended up in this traumatic situation. The fact is you have to be honest with yourself about the answers to these questions. Otherwise, you forfeit the right to get back on track with your destiny.

When I resigned from Haven Baptist, I made a promise I would not go back to another Baptist church. I told myself I was going to start my own church in California where I could do what I believed God was calling me to do. In 2012, right after Hurricane Sandy, I had to go to San Diego for business. I also took Kim with me. The moment we walked out of the airport we sensed this was the place we would eventually call home. Now, I've travelled to over thirty states, and I have never had that feeling before. This was totally different; I had no doubt this would be home. What struck us the most in San Diego was the homeless population. We wondered how such a beautiful place can have so many homeless people suffering. We wanted to do something about it; we knew we couldn't entirely eradicate the problem, but we wanted to come as close as possible. After our week ended, we knew we would be back.

The eight months I had off from pastoring was a time of rest, a time to reflect on how far I had come and consider some of the mistakes I had made. It was much-needed time. During those eight months I traveled, served as a guest minister at other churches, and released my second book. So, I wasn't just hanging around and waiting for things to fall into my lap. I was working toward something bigger than me.

One day in late November, a friend informed me the pastor of Hartford Baptist Church was planning on leaving by the end of the year. I called one of my contacts at Hartford Baptist, named Jasmine. She confirmed this information was true. Jasmine also said I should apply to be the interim pastor. I figured Hartford Baptist wouldn't want me because I don't have a master's degree in divinity (MDiv) or a doctorate. I didn't feel I was qualified. Plus, I was moving to California by the end of the year, so it wouldn't make sense to apply. Jasmine suggested I pray about it.

I talked to my wife about this potential move. My wife was over Baptist churches in general, so she wasn't excited about the idea of me joining another one. I also suggested we pray about it and see what God said. She agreed, and we started praying.

A few weeks later, Jasmine called me to say that she knew I wanted to move out west but hoped I would consider becoming their interim pastor. By mid-December I sent in my résumé. I interviewed and was hired in February 2019. I was grateful for the opportunity to pastor again. Even though it was an interim position, I gave it my all. When COVID-19 sent us into lockdown, God blessed me to keep the church going through prayer, fasting, and inspirational messages. On Sundays and during the week I made it my business to exemplify good leadership and lend biblical advice to the deacon board.

Despite all of this, I still had the West Coast on my mind. No matter how successful the church was, I always felt drawn to California. Many of the church members asked me whether I was going to apply to be the senior pastor. I would tell them I was there until God sent their new pastor. Week after week, people from the congregation would ask me the same question, and I would continue to give them the same answer. Jasmine would call me every now and then with the same question. She would tell me she thought I was in a good place and the people liked me. Ultimately, I felt pressured to apply for something I really didn't want.

As I stated earlier, people will try to influence you to do what is safe. The thing is, the safe option can cost you your life. I asked Kimberlee what she thought. She was ready to move to California but thought this could be a good experience. It was an established church, and we believed the board operated with integrity.

I decided to give it a shot and reluctantly applied. I placed what had been important to me on the back burner. Does that sound familiar? Doing what others want and becoming a version of their desires instead of your own? A new vicious cycle had come into play all because I didn't follow through on what I knew in my heart to be better for me and my family. I had to convince myself to believe Hartford Baptist was where I was supposed to be when, deep down, I knew better.

If you have to lie to yourself about what you know is not true, you are in a complicated place in your life. Think for a moment about all those times you felt something nudging you and that small voice was saying, "This is not for you." Maybe you were offered a position but something inside you kept yelling out that you shouldn't take it. But because you were afraid of being uncomfortable, you made temporary positions permanent. Fear will have you accept something that's beneath you all because you haven't realized how valuable you are.

Know you are worth more than a weekly paycheck. You are worth more than the pennies an employer tries to lure you in with. You are worth more. There is more to life than punching in and punching out. There is more to life than building someone else's vision. There is greatness in you, and the sooner you realize and accept it, the further you will go in life.

Honesty and integrity can cost you!

This book in no way, shape, or form is political. My ultimate goal is to make sure the people who read these stories are inspired to move forward despite trauma they have experienced. With that being said, I would like to highlight someone I believe has stood for honesty and integrity.

Republican Congresswoman Liz Cheney represented Wyoming's at-large congressional district from January 2019 to

May 2021. She had been in Congress since 2017 and was the Republican Conference chairperson, the third-highest-ranking Republican in the House of Representatives. She has been and continues to be a fierce and open critic of former President Trump. Though I may not agree with all of Representative Cheney's policies, I have to stand with her in regards to her stance around "the Big Lie." As many know, former President Trump claimed the 2020 presidential election was stolen from him. Even before the 2020 election took place, he was spreading lies about massive voter fraud despite zero evidence.

Representative Cheney was one of few Republicans who stood up for the truth and the Constitution. On January 6, 2021, two months after the election, the former president held a rally down the street from the Capitol building, still spewing his lies about the election. His words of division and hate energized his base, contributing to an invasion of the Capitol by right-wing, QAnon conspiracy theorists and others. It was an outlandish attack on democracy; at least seven people died in connection with the riot and many were injured. All of this took place because the former president wanted to stop the certification of Joe Biden, a president different than him, as the newest president of the United States.

Some Republicans were moved enough by their consciences to speak out about the atrocity that took place at the Capitol. But as time went on, many refused to denounce the actions of the former president from fear of losing votes. Turning their backs on the Constitution, and their integrity, was more important than admitting Donald Trump was responsible for the attack on the Capitol. Liz Cheney was among a mere few who spoke out about the former president's role on

January 6, 2021, and was one of ten Republicans who voted to impeach Donald Trump for inciting the mob.

This did not sit well with her Republican colleagues. Once they realized Representative Cheney could not be bullied into supporting a lie, they retaliated. On Wednesday, May 12, 2021, the Republican leadership in the House voted to remove Cheney from her leadership role. Instead of backing down, immediately after the vote, Representative Cheney said, "I will do everything I can to ensure that the former president never again gets anywhere near the Oval Office."

No matter what you think about Representative Cheney's politics, you can admire how, when her own party turned against her, she continued to stand for what she believed in and navigate through the storm. I use Representative Cheney as an example of one who values her morals and the rule of law. She refused to compromise her integrity for a position; her commitment to the truth cost her a leadership role in the party, but she has managed to continue to be influential. Standing up for what's right isn't always easy but it's always worth it in the end.

During the height of the COVID-19 pandemic, I would occasionally meet with the deacons of Hartford Baptist, sometimes virtually and other times in person at the church. My presence at the meetings was to lend godly advice to keep structure in the church until the election of a new senior pastor. For a while, the meetings were successful. We were all of one accord and it seemed things were getting better for the church. That is, until there was an issue regarding appointing new officers and ordaining a deacon.

I informed the board I thought it was good they were considering moving forward but I cautioned them not to appoint people to positions until a new pastor had been selected. Some of the members of the board, including the chairman of trustees, Ernest Smith, wanted to know why they should wait. I explained that not only were we in a global pandemic but they should give the new pastor an opportunity to select their team. I also suggested the church and the officers needed to be in prayer about who would be the new pastor. I went on to say it was unwise to start appointing people when the physical church was still closed to in-person services.

You could feel the tension in the air after I spoke. Trustee Smith asked how long I expected them to wait. I reiterated that they had to wait on God and give the new pastor an opportunity to get to know the people they would be shepherding. At that point everyone got quiet. The chairman of deacons, Brother Slaughter, said they had a deacon-in-training who needed to be ordained and asked if I would ordain him. I said "no," that was not my role as the interim pastor. The role of the interim pastor is to preach and teach the gospel of Jesus Christ, conduct funerals, baptize, and marry. I made it clear I would not be ordaining anyone.

Deacon Scott pointed out that they had a Christian education department position to fill and I had helped interview those candidates. I responded that while that was true, after much prayer and fasting I had concluded it would be in the best interests of the church if the deacons waited on the new pastor. In the interim, we could continue with what we'd been doing. I would continue to preach and teach online and have our weekly time of prayer. This would be sufficient until we saw how we would navigate through this new normal.

I could tell the board was not happy with the stance I was taking. After that meeting, they never asked for my advice again. Instead, they started to pay ministers an hourly rate of $250 to give them advice and tell them what they wanted to hear. They were so adamant about putting people into positions they would do whatever it took to get me out of the way so they could do what they wanted to do. My relationship with the board was no longer the same because my commitment to the ministry was far more important than pleasing others. I was now a marked man.

The board started plotting ways to get rid of me, but they had a hard time because I was leading with integrity. Deacons would try and start unnecessary arguments just to see if I would blow up, but I ignored them. Deacon Scott started calling different pastors and even called some of the deacons from Haven Baptist to try and throw mud on my name. They were coming after me hard. I couldn't understand why they were so upset about receiving godly advice. Then it all came to me: I knew that Deacon Scott was sleeping with the woman he wanted to become the Christian education director. The deacon-in-training believed if he could get ordained, he would have more authority in the church. It was no longer about ministry; it was about occupying positions people weren't qualified to have.

That's some of the twisted shit that goes on in God's house, and if you don't comply, they will fuck you over in the name of the Lord. Don't get me wrong; not all churches are like the ones I am describing. There are many that really want to serve the community and glorify God. Then you have others that think they own God's house and have a warped sense of reality. As I have said before, this is all about maintaining control. For some it's not about a calling. Their real motive is to have power and influence. Their agenda is more important than God's.

They continued to apply the pressure by nitpicking about how the morning service would flow. Every time I turned around the chairman of deacons would be in my face making stupid remarks about the service. He would ask, for instance, if we had changed the order of the service without his permission. I would just look at him, take a deep breath, and explain the service had been the same since we reopened but he was free to change it if he wanted to. I often had to walk away to control my anger. He tried and tried but still couldn't provoke me. Thankfully for the deacon I was in therapy, so I was able to control my anger. However, if this was pre-therapy, it unfortunately would have been a completely different outcome.

After being there for almost thirteen months, I went to Trustee Smith and Deacon Slaughter to discuss a raise. That was their opportunity to fully fuck with me. After they deliberated for over a month, they came back with an evaluation form that they got from another pastor. In the evaluation form they claimed I needed to improve on my preaching and teaching. They said that if I wanted a day off, my paycheck would be docked so they could pay another preacher to take my place for that Sunday. They added that my all-around performance needed work. I read that shit and thought to myself, *These motherfuckers are high off their own supply. I have been here for fourteen months, kept the church alive through a church split and a global pandemic, by the help of God, and this is the stunt they are trying to pull.*

The church had begun to flourish under my leadership, and now they wanted to criticize my work. To add insult to injury they wanted to give me a two-percent raise when they knew they could do more. I asked both Trustee Smith and Deacon Slaughter if one of their children showed them this contract would they then tell them to sign it. Neither answered. I asked if either one of them would sign it. Complete silence! I explained that what they were presenting was an insult to the work I had done. I asked if they had involved the church with this decision. Trustee Smith said the church had put them in charge to handle business. That was not the question I had asked, so I repeated my question. Neither Deacon Slaughter nor Trustee Smith could answer my question.

Finally, I said, "This has nothing to do with my performance as a minister. This is personal because I refuse to ordain a deacon and install a Christian education director." I told them I would not be signing the new contract and would be in prayer about my next move. I knew what they wrote about me in that farce of an evaluation had nothing to do with the real value of my work. Their actions were personal.

To be honest, I couldn't figure out why I was so upset because I knew this role was supposed to be temporary. I guess I was more humiliated than anything else. I felt abused, neglected, and taken advantage of. For a few weeks I thought about exposing what they were doing to the entire church. I wanted them to be hurt the way I was hurt. But all that would have done was divide the church even more, and that was not my intention.

Instead, I prayed. I exercised. I cursed. And I prayed some more. I knew what I had to do. I removed myself from the list of candidates and shared with them I was no longer interested in being the senior pastor.

You would've thought that had been sufficient. They went a step further and decided to terminate my contract on my day off. They planned a secret meeting and agreed to fire me without cause. I was surprisingly relieved. The fact is I knew I didn't belong there and this was only supposed to be temporary. But when you put your all into something or someone and it is abruptly taken away, you experience trauma from being violated without cause. I must admit, I wanted to seek revenge because I had gone into this position with no hidden agenda, no secret plan. All I wanted to do was serve God's people to the best of my ability. I wanted to minister to them so they would see there is joy on the other side of all the pain. Instead, I was blindsided by people who had their own agenda in God's house. I was attacked because I led with integrity and honesty. Though I think the outcome could have been handled better, I continue to stand on the fact that I did the best I could with what I had. I know God has major plans for me, and I will not allow a little setback to hold me back from my purpose.

All of us will go through some sort of humiliating scenario where we wish we can change the outcome. The fact is you cannot change something that was meant to teach you a lesson. Hartford Baptist proved I didn't have to go off to get my point across, but even when you are calm you can still be treated unfairly. So, I say to those of you struggling with questions like, *Why did this happen to me?*, struggle no more, and be thankful, because it couldn't have happened to a better person. You are designed to handle the pressure, because through all of that you are still standing, and you will continue to stand if you stand on integrity and honesty.

All organizations have power struggles. Some are not as intense as others; however, they are there. With churches, it all depends on how long they have allowed toxic behavior to run rampant through the institution. When going into a pastoral position in a church, you must go in with these questions: How long have they been without a pastor? Has the church gone through a split? Are there any power struggles between board and pastor? And lastly, you have to ask who has the final say, the pastor or the deacon board? Those questions are needed to determine the dynamic of the church—not so much with corporate America.

Just when I thought I had found my sweet spot

My wife, Kimberlee, has a bachelor's degree in psychology and is pursuing another bachelor's degree in information technology. This woman is brilliant. She can take a malfunctioning computer, an Apple watch, or any other electronic and, within minutes, it's working. There is nothing she cannot do; whatever she puts her mind to, she always makes it happen.

Just before Kim and I started dating, she got offered a job to work for a telecommunications company, Company A. Kim was excited to work there. They treated their employees well and paid them handsomely. Things were moving in the right direction for her. There was also talk of her taking on more of a managerial role soon. Things were going well. Then the recession hit and Kim was laid off. She was crushed. It seemed like the moment she started to flourish, her wings were clipped.

After a few months of being unemployed, a temp agency reached out to Kim for an open role in the same company she was just laid off from. We talked about the position and what it would mean for her future. She decided to take it. Kim really worked hard. She was learning a lot and the supervisors were pleased with her performance, so much so she was rehired on a permanent basis. We couldn't believe the irony of it all. It felt like a rollercoaster ride with surprise twists and turns.

Her career was going well, we had our first child, and we got married. Things were looking up. Then, out of the blue, Company A merged with Company B. Many of the jobs were being taken over by Company B. Kim's job was safe, so we didn't worry too much about the merger. Later in the year, Company A received an email that the New York location (where Kim worked) was closing, and the new location would be in California, the Bay Area. Not only was the location closing but the employees had to reapply for their jobs and there was no guarantee they would be rehired for their positions at the new location.

We were devastated by the news. Just when we thought we had hit a sweet spot, here came another blow. Kim decided she would not reapply for a job she already had so she accepted the severance package. I really felt bad for my wife; I felt helpless. There was nothing I could do for her, and that was stressful. Kim was depressed because she thought she had finally found a place she belonged and would have the opportunity to move up. Life is interesting that way. One moment you are flying high and the next, often without any fault of your own, the wind is knocked out of you. It's not like Kim wasn't doing a great job; it was because Company B already had who they wanted to fill certain roles and some of the people from Company A just didn't fit the criteria. When people are trying to get rid of you, they will come up with all sorts of excuses why you are not qualified for the position or will continue to move the goal line out of your reach. When those things happen in your life it chips away at your confidence; it eats away at your self-worth. But you have to be strong.

Being laid off for the second time sent Kim into a real dark place. She had a hard time being motivated, her drive and passion subsided, and she couldn't seem to find her way out. Our marriage suffered; her physical and mental health suffered. Drinking was her comfort, and sleep was the highlight of her day. We argued constantly and barely spent time together because of my busy travel schedule. There were moments I no longer wanted to be married and she no longer wanted to live. Our life of happiness turned into a life of bickering. Every day was a new argument. We were drifting apart.

I didn't know how to help Kim through her pain, and she had no idea how to navigate through that troubling time in her life. It was a mess. One night we argued so intensely it scared our two young children. We yelled, screamed, cursed one another out, and took off our wedding rings. We were sick of fighting and sick of being broke. Then we looked at both of our children and thought, *What the hell are we doing?* The next day we talked and made a commitment to work things out. Not just for the kids but for ourselves as well. We didn't want to get divorced; we loved one another and were determined to make it. That's the thing: you have to want to make things work. You have to be determined to see it through, and that was our mentality. Things started to get better. We started to communicate, and when things bothered us, we didn't let it build up, we dealt with it before it got out of control. As time went on, Kim found another job in a field she didn't particularly care for even though she had the experience. She took it to be of help to her family, but it was of no help to her mentally.

I'm doing this for my family

"I'm doing this for my family" is a phrase we use because we feel it is what others want to hear. *I'm going to get this job that I hate because I love my family. I'm going to endure and suffer through the disrespect that comes my way so that I can provide for my family. I'll stay late and work with no overtime because I don't want to get fired for speaking up for myself. And how would I provide for my family with no job?*

We are belittled, overlooked, underpaid, stepped on, all because we have been programmed to accept what is offered to provide for our family. No one thinks about why they are so tired when they think they slept eight hours, but in reality tossed and turned all night. No one understands why they are so frustrated when they have a steady job. No one sees that they are burned out by going to a job they despise and receiving a check that, once they've paid all their bills, only has a few dollars left to carry them through to the next paycheck. People live with this reality every day. We drag ourselves out of bed every morning just to collapse back into the same bed every night. We are dying on the inside just to provide for our families on the outside.

That's where Kimberlee found herself, accepting a job at Company C. On the outside it appeared to be a booming company that invested in its employees. Since we had only one income coming in, Kim decided to accept the position. During the early years of our marriage we struggled financially because of continued layoffs and massive salary cuts in my company. There would be times we could barely make rent and would run out of food. No one knew of our struggles; we kept it to ourselves believing things would eventually work out.

While Kimberlee was interviewing for Company C, there was another person who was interviewing, a white woman named Maureen, who was much younger and had less experience. Kimberlee and Maureen were applying for the same position, which had two openings. They both interviewed and were offered the job. Kim was hired on a temporary basis and Maureen on a full-time basis with benefits. At that time, Kim had ten years of experience in this field. Maureen had none and yet was offered the full-time position. Meanwhile, Kim had to prove herself before being offered the full-time position as well. Ain't that some shit? But because she wanted to contribute to the family finances, she swallowed her pride and accepted the temp role. Talk about a humongous blow to your ego and self-worth. When Kim told me what she was going through I felt helpless and mad. My amazing and talented wife was being treated terribly and there was nothing I could do about it. I knew she was unhappy, but she refused to quit. Kim is so resilient. She is stronger than she gives herself credit for. My wife is an example of strength and determination, and when it's all said and done, I know she can conquer anything she sets her mind to.

After being there for two months, Kim was offered the full-time position with Company C. I guess they finally saw she was more than qualified to handle the workload. Five months later, they fired Maureen because of her inability to do the work. Isn't it interesting the person Company C was holding back turned out to be the one they needed and Maureen was the one they should've kept as a temp? Kim worked at Company C for four years. During that time, she worked hard and excelled in her role.

When opportunities came for Kim to get promoted, her supervisor would block any attempts for her to advance. Kim couldn't understand. She was doing everything right. Every time Kim applied for a new role she would be denied, even though she met the qualifications for every role she applied for. This continued for years until she finally checked out. Kim did what most of us have done at some point, and that is stop trying. When you continue to keep hitting a wall, you eventually tap out. The pain becomes so overwhelming, and the humiliation of rejection crushes your spirit. Kim could have easily quit but she stuck it out because we started to finally get our heads above water.

Kim's last year at Company C was really bad. Her self-worth suffered and our marriage started to get off track again. Kim's old boss had moved to another role and, instead of promoting within, they hired someone who worked at the Apple store. Yes, she was another white woman with no experience in management or the field of interest. One of Kimberlee's colleagues, Jessica, a Black woman, applied for the role and was turned down. Jessica had the experience and the degree, but they refused to consider her as a manager. After they hired the white woman, the company wanted Jessica to train her. Jessica refused and quit. She told Kimberlee she would no longer be disrespected by a company that didn't see her worth.

Somehow Jessica wasn't good enough for the role but was experienced enough to train someone for it.

For the next twelve months Kim dealt with the new manager who had no clue what she was doing. Not only was she incompetent, but she was also a pain in Kim's ass. One morning Kim arrived five minutes late. When she got to her cubicle the new manager spun around in Kim's chair and said, "Good morning! Welcome to work!" Kim looked her square in the face and responded, "You are in my seat." Her manager got up and walked off. Kim was furious! She called and told me what happened. She said, "Babe, this bitch has lost her mind; I don't know how much more I can take. But I am going to stick it out for our family."

One day Kim had finally had enough and decided to start looking for another job closer to home. Kim's last few months at Company C were awful. Her manger started to nitpick her work and monitor when she would arrive, what time she took for lunch, and when she left for the day. Kim's working environment was toxic, but she pressed on.

The winters in Connecticut are either hit or miss; it can be mild or there can be two feet of snow. You just never know. There would be times when our kids' school would close due to a snowstorm and Kim would need to work from home. Kim explained this to her manager, who wasn't receptive but had no other choice but to accept it. That year was a tough winter, so Kim had to work from home most days, and that didn't sit well with her manager. She started to complain that Kim was working too much from home and needed to start coming in whether it snowed or not. This caused Kim a lot of anxiety to the point where she was losing weight and losing sleep.

While the kids were on winter break Kim took a week off to decompress and reevaluate her life. While she was off, she interviewed at Company D, which so happened to be up the street from our home. The interview went well and the hiring team told Kim they would get back to her within a week. That Sunday night, before Kim went back to work, she started to get sick and feel anxious. She didn't sleep the entire night. That morning I sensed she was unhappy about going back to Company C. I told her if she wanted to leave, I would support her, especially since she was a shoo-in for the new job she had just interviewed for.

Kim arrived at work at 9 a.m. and her manager was sitting at her desk again. She told Kim she needed to speak with her about her performance. They went to a conference room and her manager gave her an awful review. Her manager went on to say that even if it was a blizzard she had to come to the office, otherwise she would be written up and after three times she would be fired. My wife sat there calmly and after her manager finished, she asked Kim to sign her review and agree to the terms. Kim said she wasn't signing anything and gave her two week's notice. When Kim told me the news, I was proud of her. She said her manager was dumbfounded. I was so happy she was getting out of that toxic place. A few days later Company D offered Kim the job. Life felt a little lighter and we celebrated Kim's new beginnings.

Enough is enough, I'm moving forward

Two weeks after her leaving Company C, Kim and I were feeling optimistic. There was a new fire in Kim's eyes; she was ready to take on the world. I was delighted to see her so happy and enthusiastic about this next chapter in her life. Just before Company D extended the offer, they shared with Kim that she would be receiving a sizable sign-on bonus based on her experience. They also shared that after a year there would be room for advancement. This was music to Kim's ears, and I was overjoyed about the great things that were happening for her.

Kim started her new job, and they were so amazed at how diligent she was and how she was able to get things done before the set deadline. Kim was putting her best foot forward. Her performance was so outstanding her colleagues would write notes to her manager, Meredith, about how much of a pleasure Kim is to work with. When it came time for her performance reviews, Kim would get a five-out-of-five company rating most of the time. The lowest she ever got was a four. Fives were unheard of, but Kim was knocking it out of the park.

As I mentioned, Kim has always been interested in IT; that is really her passion. So when opportunities would become available for her to take on IT-related roles, she would apply. Unfortunately, she would never be considered. After a few times of being denied promotions, Kim went to the hiring managers and asked them why she wasn't being considered. They tried to hem and haw with their answers, but Kim was relentless. They finally told her that her manager, Meredith, was the one standing in her way.

Kim was shocked; she couldn't believe Meredith was the one behind all her rejections. As you can imagine this was a major blow to Kim's confidence. She approached Meredith and asked her why she was blocking her opportunity to advance her career. Meredith told her, based upon her reviews, she was not ready for a promotion. This was confusing because, as I said, Kim would get no less than a four and most of the time a five. Kim was livid. She pointed out that what Meredith was saying wasn't true. She reminded Meredith that she had excelled in every performance review and everyone she worked with had stated in writing how she met every deadline ahead of time. Finally, Meredith said, "You have to be with the company for a certain amount of time before being promoted." Kim pushed back, saying that both Meredith and HR had told Kim she had to be at the company at least a year to be promoted. She had already been there for more than a year. Meredith avoided responding to this and told Kim they would discuss this again at her next review. Kim was upset about this blatant disrespect. After that it was hard for her to be motivated, but she kept on because she wanted to contribute to the family finances.

Shortly after Kim started at Company D, a young lady named Kathleen was hired. Kathleen was a young white woman with no experience, and she always showed up late. As a matter of fact, Kathleen would call in sick every Monday because she was so hung over from the weekend. It got so bad that Kathleen would ask to work from home to take her cat to the veterinarian or simply to stay home if her cat wasn't feeling well. Meredith would consistently permit Kathleen to work from home, but if Kim asked to work from home because one of the children was sick or it had snowed, Meredith would complain. Kim continued to apply for promotions and was consistently denied. This was another dark moment for my wife. No matter how hard she worked, no matter how many compliments and outstanding reviews she received, she was still denied what was rightfully hers. Kathleen, on the other hand, became Meredith's favorite. Kathleen could do no wrong in Meredith's eyes. She could show up at 10 a.m. and leave at 3 p.m. and Meredith wouldn't say anything. This was very frustrating for Kim to deal with and it opened up old wounds that weren't fully healed yet.

What was happening to my brilliant wife was traumatizing, and she didn't deserve this treatment. Kim is a hard worker, dedicated mother, and faithful wife. Why did it seem like the world was turning against her? Why was every company denying her what she earned? No one could give us any answers. Not only did this happen to Kim, I know it has happened to countless others who have put their time in, gone to school, and worked the long hours, just to be humiliated over and over again. Consistent mistreatment can tear away at your ability to believe in yourself. Being told you don't have what it takes locks you in a prison of shame. Every time you try to escape, the shame paralyzes you from moving forward. After a while you stop trying; you give up and succumb to what people and your circumstances tell you. Then there is nothing left. My wife was heading in that direction.

I tried my best to encourage Kim, but I didn't know how miserable she was feeling. It was bad. Just when you thought it couldn't get worse, it did. Kathleen had been with the company for just over a year and applied for a promotion. Mind you, all of Kathleen's colleagues complained about her work performance. They shared how disappointed they were when the deadline for a project had passed and Kathleen hadn't contributed her portion. Many of the team members had expressed concerns about Kathleen's behavior, but it fell on deaf ears. After Kathleen applied for her promotion, Meredith made it her priority to prepare Kathleen for her interview. They had mock interviews during lunch and Meredith even had Kim doing some of Kathleen's work as Kathleen prepped for the upcoming interview. How demeaning could they be? Kim stuck it out just to be there for her family. After several weeks, the company announced Kathleen had received a promotion and would be moving to another location. Kathleen was provided with a sizable raise and moving allowance to help her relocate to Ohio. Kim was a wreck! I couldn't comfort her. No words of affirmation could help my wife, who was hurting deep down inside. She would put on a brave face every day but her soul was tired.

About a week later, Company D announced that they would be merging with Company E. Meredith was laid off and Kim received a lateral move with a few extra dollars added to her check. Kim was now reporting to Natalie. Natalie is a Black woman from the West Indies and a former corporate attorney. We thought Kim would finally be able to get ahead. Boy, were we wrong. Natalie was worse. She was condescending, disrespectful, and uptight. For the last time Kimberlee tried to apply for a promotion and was denied again. When Natalie found out Kim was applying for other positions, she would tell the company not to offer them to her because she wouldn't be a good fit.

When Kim and Natalie would have their one-on-ones, Natalie would try to belittle Kim and tell her she needed to step her game up. Kim told her about her stellar performance and asked what the real issue was. Natalie said the information about her performance was news to her because Meredith would tell Natalie that Kim was never at her desk and her work was subpar. Kim told Natalie to look through her file and see for herself. Natalie found out that Kim was telling the truth about her performance reviews and about how her team members felt about her. You would have thought that would have been sufficient, but it wasn't. Natalie was still determined to bring Kim down.

One day I saw the pain and disappointment in Kim's eyes. I asked her what she wanted to do. She said she wanted to quit and go back to school for IT. I told her I loved her and would support her. The next day Kim gave her two week's notice. When my wife got home you could see the joy in her eyes and feel the change in her attitude. After taking a few months off to get herself together, she applied to school and was admitted to a program to earn a bachelor's degree in information technology. I am so proud of my wife for how she stepped out in faith. She trusted God and believed in herself, and things began moving in the right direction for my baby!

Throughout this chapter I have made several references to Kim sticking things out for her family. I did that to show how many of us are stuck because of too much commitment to others and not enough to ourselves. I am not saying abandon your responsibilities as a parent and a spouse—take care of your children and be there for your partner. What I am saying is if your job is making you sick and putting a strain on your spouse and children then you need to make a major decision. Sometimes those tough decisions will help your family to see how important it is to take care of yourself and not overdo it. Imagine if we started showing our families we don't have to stay in a career that's draining us of our creativity to provide for our children. How about we change the narrative? What if we stepped out in faith to prove to our families that there is a way to be happy and productive in careers that can financially support us and our children? It's time to change the strategy and prove there is something better out there if you believe in yourself and step out. You got this, and I believe in you.

For me, stepping out in faith was being intentional about changing my narrative. I did that by refusing to accept what people believed I should have. I was determined to follow my dreams no matter the cost.

One key thing is important: you must have confidence in yourself. I cannot stress that enough. Believe you have the ability to do anything you set your mind to. There will be times when you will be disappointed and suffer setbacks; that is a part of life. The key is refusing to give up, refusing to settle for less! Push forward no matter what, and eventually you will achieve all that you are working toward.

7

The Trauma of Rejection

It Takes Courage and Curiosity to Keep Going

Journalist Michelle Miller of CBS News interviewed the living-legend dancer Ms. Debbie Allen. In her interview, Debbie shared about how the trauma of rejection still haunts her to this day. When Debbie was sixteen years old, she applied and auditioned for the North Carolina School of the Arts. Her family was extremely proud of her and looking forward to receiving the phone call of her being accepted into the school.

Yet the teacher in charge made it clear Debbie was not the right body type to be a dancer. What a painful experience to go through at such an impressionable age. Young Debbie felt like a failure; she believed she let her family down. When she arrived back home, her mother told her she had failed. Years later, Debbie realized her mother's words were not meant to harm or disparage her but to help her get back on track. It taught her responsibility and made her work even harder to pursue her dreams. Michelle Miller also pointed out that Debbie's mother took the banister from the staircase, nailed it to the ground, and that became her barre to practice on. The gut-wrenching experience of being rejected was no excuse to stop practicing; if anything, it pushed her even harder.

After being rejected from the North Carolina School of the Arts, Debbie went to Howard University, where she earned a bachelor's of fine arts. During her freshman year, Debbie gave up on her dream of being a dancer until one night she was at a party, where she was dancing the night away. A man named Mike Malone approached her and told her she could really dance. That night Mike showed Debbie a picture of himself in *Dance Magazine*. That was the moment her passion for dance was reignited again. Mike asked Debbie to join his dance company, and she was off to New York to follow her dreams of being a dancer.[1]

There are times when all you need is to see a picture of what you can be, and the rest is history. Debbie later became the first Black woman to win a Golden Globe for a TV series. She has choreographed the Oscars ten times; been nominated for twenty Emmys, and won three; and founded the Debbie Allen Dance Academy. She has been a Kennedy Center honoree, actor,

---

1. https://podcasts.apple.com/co/podcast/arts-legend-debbie-allen-on-her-groundbreaking-career/id1157631148?i=1000546581054.

director, producer, dancer, and choreographer. There is nothing this amazing woman can't do. The rejection she faced at the age of sixteen prepared her for an extraordinary life. It would've been easy for Debbie to give up and allow that teacher from the University of North Carolina School of the Arts to detract her from her passion. Instead, she got back on track. She used her mother's words and her teacher's rejection to fall back in love with her true calling.

In life, you cannot avoid the negativity that will come your way. You cannot avoid criticism; eventually you will have to come face to face with it. You have a choice to either let rejection and negativity hold you down or to take away their strength and stand your ground. If you continue to see something greater in yourself, then you will have what it takes to conquer every mountain you encounter.

There is a certain level of confidence that is necessary to keep going. An internal dialogue between you and yourself is essential, because often we are the very ones who reject our own greatness. We talk ourselves out of what we know we can do out of fear of what someone else will say about our decisions. To add insult to injury, we seem to forget what we've done for other people and organizations and think there is no way we can do it for ourselves. The truth is, we can most certainly accomplish what we set our minds to. The trick is to reject the negativity we continuously invite into our minds. Negative energy has no place in our thoughts. Negative energy destroys our creativity and incarcerates our innovation.

Blocking negative energy doesn't mean you won't have to endure some days of being uncomfortable. What it means is that you must never be the one totally responsible for everything going wrong in your life. You have to be the one to create a productive atmosphere so that all of the negatives will have no opportunity to diminish all of the positives happening in your life.

My wife, Kimberlee, signed up our two oldest children, Brendan and Sasha, for soccer. One night at the dinner table, Brendan asked me if I was coming to his soccer tryouts. I told him I would be there. Sasha asked the same question and I assured both of them I would be present cheering them on. Brendan then interjected and said, "I probably won't do well anyway." I snapped at my son, telling him to never say that again. I told him he would be just fine and that if he gave it his best shot, he would be amazed at what he accomplished. Then it was like a ripple effect. Sasha announced that she's not good at soccer. I was getting annoyed. I asked them both where they were getting this from. I told them neither one of them had tried out yet and already they were counting themselves out. I encouraged Brendan and Sasha to do their best and all would be well.

Then I began to think about how so many adults do the same thing. We conclude that we are not going to make it, and that sets the negativity train in motion. We reject our ability to do something extraordinary and belittle our gifts and talents. If you do that often enough you will project that same energy on to your children, and they will do it to their children. Then you will have generations of people who are miserable because they didn't have enough courage to see that they have what it takes to be exceptional. When you reject your authentic self, you reject all the good things you bring to the table. If you reject yourself over and over again, you will miss out on the joys of making a significant impact in the world.

One of the most unattractive things people do is talk disparagingly about themselves. You cannot say you should have been further along than where you are right now if you are the one laying the bricks of defeat. Ask yourself what you are doing that is causing a delay in what you want your life to be. Once you have figured out the issue, secure a solution so that you won't have to have that conversation with yourself again.

I've had these struggles in my own life; however, when I left my home church, I made it my priority to speak words of affirmation into my life. When I did that consistently, things changed. I would meet new people who aligned with my work ethic and values. When I noticed the change, I maintained that same energy. I suggest using that same strategy, and I believe it will work for you as well.

Move in silence

Moving in silence is something my mother taught me a long time ago. She never said those words, but she implied them. When my mother was trying to move from the U.K. to the U.S., she shared this information with some of her sisters. Their response was not what she expected. They asked her what she was going to do when she got there and where she was going to live. They told her she would be better off if she stayed in London. All that negativity came at her all at once. Her takeaway? From now on, keep your mouth shut. When you are trying to make certain moves in your life and accomplish great things, sometimes you have to keep quiet. If there is a task that has never been done before in your family you may have to move swiftly and silently. Because the moment the wrong person hears about your plans, they are going to try to rain on your parade.

Once the United States approved my mom's permanent residency application, we were on our way. I believe it was a Saturday afternoon when we left for New York, and I wanted to know if we were going to say "goodbye" to everyone. My mother looked at me and told me to keep my mouth shut. I didn't understand it then, but I am grateful that I do now. How many times have you shared something with a friend or family member about what you wanted to accomplish and they bombarded you with a whole lot of "whys" and "how comes"? I'm pretty sure it was very frustrating. Now think about if you had listened to their negativity; you would have been living in regret because the people you shared your dream with couldn't see what you already knew to be true. The fact is they can't see it because the vision or idea didn't come to them, it came to you. But you have to have the courage and discipline to follow your dreams. The courage to start, and the discipline to continue.

My mother had the courage to apply for a green card, and when it came, we moved. The discipline piece was when times got hard, she kept working. She believed America was where she wanted to be and was determined to make it work. No matter how many people told her she couldn't, she continued to remind herself she could. Having faith in yourself gives you the ability to excel over your naysayers and reach for the stars. There's a popular saying: "Shoot for the moon. Even if you miss, you'll land among the stars."

I regret that I accepted their rejection of who I wanted to be

When I was in high school, I was not a particularly good student. I struggled in some of my classes and was somewhat awkward in the social arena. I know you are probably thinking, "Who wasn't?" But I really struggled to make friends, and math class used to kick my butt. It was not an enjoyable time in my life.

That is, until one day when I saw a student walk by with a blue uniform on that had several medals attached. I mean, he was sharp. Shoes polished, white shirt crisp and clean, and his navy-blue suit was flawless. I made a U-turn and followed him to his class. It turned out to be the Air Force Reserve Officers' Training Corps (ROTC) class. When I walked in, I was met by an older Black man dressed in the same suit. He looked at me and asked if he could help me. I asked what the class was about and he told me it was for students interested in pursuing a career in the United States Air Force. His name was Sergeant Pugh, and he suggested I hurry on to class before the bell rang. That day all I could think about was how I could get into that class. The next morning, I arrived at school around 7 a.m. and happened to see Sergeant Pugh getting out of his car. I asked him how I could join the class and he told me I had to talk to my guidance counselor. I took off running upstairs to the guidance counselor's office and waited for my counselor to arrive. When she finally came in, I told her I wanted to join ROTC because I liked the way they dress and thought I could learn a lot. She said she would add it to my schedule but I would have to make sure to attend all of my classes.

The next day I was fitted for an ROTC uniform. I felt so proud, like I finally belonged to something great. Don't get me wrong; it was hard work. We had to do drills and learn about aerospace, and if we were late, we had to do laps. I didn't care; I enjoyed it so much that as the years went on, I was promoted to second lieutenant. I excelled in that class and earned an A+ each year. ROTC taught me to have pride in myself and the work I do. It was the best thing that could ever have happened to me.

Unfortunately, two years before I graduated, Roosevelt High School terminated the program. I was devastated. The one thing I loved about school was taken away without notice. I couldn't believe all the hard work had come to an end with no warning or explanation. I cried when I found out the program was dissolved. I thought it was unfair to strip students of such a beneficial program.

The last two years of school were rough for me. I fell back into depression and barely made it out of high school. Every day I wondered what would've happened if the school had kept the ROTC program. I knew I would have been promoted to captain, or even lieutenant colonel, by the time I was supposed to graduate. There was so much I could have accomplished but it was stripped away.

After graduation I was lost; I didn't know what to do next. I held jobs for maybe six months at a time, then I would end up being fired. I was going around in a circle until I decided to join the Air Force. It was a Monday afternoon when I walked into the Air Force recruiting office. The men and women in that office reminded me of when I first saw the ROTC students walking in the hallway at Roosevelt High School. I felt at home, among my people. The recruiting officer took my information and told me I needed to take the Armed Services Vocational Aptitude Battery (ASVAB) test. After I passed the test my recruiting officer gave me a date for my physical and the day I would leave for boot camp.

When I got home, I called my sister Rae and told her the news. She was not excited, but I didn't care. Then I told my mother, and she started to scream and cry and said they were going to kill and poison me. Even though I knew she was exaggerating, I didn't understand what was going on. This was what I wanted to do with my life, and I felt my family should be happy for me. Every day my mother and sister kept badgering me about not joining the Air Force. Nonstop, all day long, it seemed I received nothing but negativity about something that made me feel whole. After about a week of hearing so much negativity I decided to withdraw my application.

To this day, I have regretted the fact that I allowed my family to reject who I wanted to be. Whenever I see military officers dressed in their uniforms, I get a little sad because I would have made a great soldier. There are times I have resentment toward my mother and sister. Then I resent myself for accepting their rejection of me. For a long time, I would do what others wanted me to do—accept positions I knew I didn't want, go places I knew I didn't want to go, all because I accepted their rejection of who I wanted to be. I am still dealing with that trauma of rejection, but each day I am getting better and making decisions that make me happy.

Since I didn't join the Air Force I focused on the ministry, but there was so much more I wanted to do than just preach on Sundays. I wanted to help people, not just spiritually but also mentally. I thought about becoming a psychologist. I figured I could help people through their emotional distress. So I started going to the library and looking things up on the internet. After reading a few books and doing my research I decided I was going to be a therapist. I ran home and told my mother I had decided to get a degree in psychology. She looked at me and laughed, saying I was not smart enough to be a psychologist. I looked at her with so much rage and bit my tongue. I turned around and walked out of the house. I got in my car and just drove. The anger I had inside me that day was like a blazing house fire. I felt angry, sad, disappointed, and defeated. But what did I do? I accepted the rejection and decided not to be myself. The trauma of rejection kept on building.

I figured since I was a minister, I should go to seminary. I told my pastor I was going to get a divinity degree. He looked at me and said, "You don't need a divinity degree, those are for crazy people."

At that point, all my confidence was gone. I felt stuck in a city and church where I no longer wanted to be. All I wanted to accomplish seemed impossible.

I wasted a few more years satisfying everyone else while my hopes of being better were crushed. I felt I was suffocating and no one cared. I saw an opportunity to become a youth pastor on Prince Edward Island, Canada. I applied, interviewed, and was offered the role. I shared this wonderful news with my mother. She got an attitude and asked what was going to happen to her when I went to Canada. I called the pastor back and turned down the job. I couldn't breathe!

Another opportunity became available to be a student pastor in California. As I was filling out the application, my mother said, "So you're just going to leave me here and go to California?" I ripped up the application and threw it in the garbage. I thought I was going to die. The trauma of rejection had sucked the life out of me. Accepting the rejection of who I wanted to be became a norm. For so many years I put my dreams on hold. I sacrificed my joy and happiness for someone else's convenience.

There are so many people who continue to hold themselves back because others' opinions have outweighed their opinions of themselves. Years go by and their dreams begin to fade away. Then one day they make up their minds that they are going to follow their dreams. No matter what anyone else says about it, they decide to do what is best for them. I recently decided to do just that.

I quit a job I hated and together with my wife decided to move across the country to California. I know not everyone will understand a decision to move a family three-thousand miles away, but I don't care about their opinion. Sometimes you must do whatever it takes to make your dreams come true. I know it's not an easy thing, but taking steps like this sure as hell is worth it. There are so many things I have learned during the pandemic. Life is short, your health is important, and you only have one chance in this world. So, therefore, you have to make it a priority to live for yourself and no one else.

People will say things to discourage you and hold you back because they don't know how to fulfill their own dreams. But don't let that stop you. Refuse to allow other people's empty words to hold you back from pursuing your heart's desire. You have what it takes to change the world, and you have what it takes to make a difference in your life. You hold the power; no one else has it unless you have relinquished it to them. Make up your mind that you will no longer allow anyone to dictate your life. Tell yourself you are qualified and capable of making things happen. You are smart enough, good enough, and strong enough to make your dreams a reality. It's time to reject someone else's rejection of who you want to be. Start now!

I don't have to take this

In the church trauma chapter of this book, I mentioned that I resigned from my first church because of my mental health. Before I resigned, I had bounced the idea off some other clergy who knew some of the issues I was dealing with at the time. When I spoke to them about it, all of them said the same thing: "Stick it out." I prayed and prayed; the more I prayed the more I knew that resigning was the right decision for me. I knew I had had enough and didn't need validation from anyone to make this decision. I did what needed to be done for my mental health. Many of the pastors were shocked by my decision. Some even sarcastically said, "Well, if that's what the Lord said then you should follow the Lord." In ministry, people will tell you to wait on the Lord or they will ask, "Did the Lord say that?" And most times that is their way to over-spiritualize everything. The Lord doesn't have to tell me to take a shower. The fact that I stink lets me know to take a shower. There are some things you just know to do. God shouldn't have to give you a sign to know it's time to do what is best for you. Common sense tells you that. I think people like to put the responsibility on God when in fact it belongs on us. I'm not saying not to pray or fast. What I am saying is that you will eventually have to make a decision or the situation will decide for you.

Leaving my church was not easy but it was necessary. It was time to go and I knew I wasn't going to take the emotional abuse any longer. It was the best decision of my life. Not many people celebrated my decision, and I am okay with that. Some wanted me to stay and fight but they were nowhere to be found when I needed support. So I took the necessary actions and it worked out for me. Rejecting what people expect of you is liberating. Accepting someone else's plan for your life is bondage and hard to escape when you have been steeped in it for so long. Take time to take care of yourself and let the chips fall where they may.

I admired the courage of tennis great Naomi Osaka when she posted a long text image on Twitter indicating that she would not participate in press conferences during the French Open, also called Roland-Garros. She stated:

> Hope you're all doing well, I'm writing this to say I'm not going to do any press during Roland Garros. I've often felt that people have no regard for athletes' mental health and this rings very true whenever I see a press conference or partake in one. We're often sat there and [...] asked questions that bring doubt into our minds and I'm just not going to subject myself to people that doubt me. I've watched many clips of athletes breaking down after a loss in the press room and I know you have as well. I believe that whole situation is kicking a person while they're down and I don't understand the reasoning behind it. Me not doing press is nothing personal to the tournament and a couple journalists have interviewed me since I was young so I have a friendly relationship with most of them. However, if the organizations think that they can just keep saying, "do press or you're gonna be fined", and

continue to ignore the mental health of the athletes that are the centerpiece of their cooperation [sic] then I just gotta laugh. Anyways, I hope the considerable amount that I get fined for this will go towards a mental health charity.[2]

Naomi's transparency was a breath of fresh air for the young and old battling mental illness. Trying to navigate through trauma is not easy, and if there are no systems in place to tackle this growing concern among athletes, we will continue to see an uprising of athletes bypassing the press. I commend Naomi for refusing to be bullied into a situation that continues to trigger her depression. Just because she is an athlete doesn't mean she hasn't battled with human emotions. No one is exempt from mental illness; it can strike at any time without warning. The fact that Naomi knew her boundaries is to be commended, not criticized. Unfortunately, several days after Naomi released her tweet, she was fined $15,000. The fine was announced in a joint statement by the organizations that run the Grand Slam tournaments—the U.S. Tennis Association, the French Tennis Federation, the All England Lawn Tennis Club, and Tennis Australia.

It is quite sad in this day and age that you can be punished if you voice your concerns about your mental health. Boundaries are created for a purpose. You may not understand it, you may even reject it, but the fact is, boundaries are there for a reason. Naomi established healthy boundaries, and I am proud of her. After she was fined, Naomi took to Instagram and said:

---

2. https://twitter.com/naomiosaka/status/1397665030015959040.

Hey everyone, this isn't a situation I ever imagined or intended when I posted a few days ago. I think now the best thing for the tournament, the other players and my well-being is that I withdraw so that everyone can get back to focusing on the tennis going on in Paris. I never wanted to be a distraction and I accept that my timing was not ideal and my message could have been clearer. More importantly I would never trivialize mental health or use the term lightly. The truth is that I have suffered long bouts of depression since the US Open in 2018 and I have had a really hard time coping with that. Anyone that knows me knows I'm intro-verted, and anyone that has seen me at the tourna-ments will notice that I'm often wearing headphones as that helps dull my social anxiety. Though the tennis press has always been kind to me (and I wanna apolo-gize especially to all the cool journalists who I may have hurt), I am not a natural public speaker and get huge waves of anxiety before I speak to the world's media. I get really nervous and find it stressful to always try to engage and give you the best answers I can. So here in Paris I was already feeling vulnerable and anxious so I thought it was better to exercise self-care and skip the press conferences. I announced it pre-emptively because I do feel like the rules are quite out-dated in parts and I wanted to highlight that. I wrote privately to the tournament apologizing and saying that I would be more than happy to speak with them after the tournament as the Slams are intense. I'm gonna take some time away from the court now, but when the time is right I really want to work with the Tour to discuss ways we can make things better for the players, press and fans. Anyways hope you are all doing well and staying safe, love you guys I'll see you when I see you.[3]

Again, it is so unfortunate how athletes that give their all to their craft feel pressured into making statements to appease people who most likely don't give a shit about them. These athletes use their bodies to make these organizations billions of dollars, and the moment they speak their truth they are penalized and treated like second-class citizens. No human being, whether they are a famous athlete or the cashier at Target, should have to endure such badgering. Personally, if I have already opened my heart and shared how a particular situation gives me anxiety, then I shouldn't be subjected to harsh ridicule. Understand where I am coming from and give me the space I need to work through my issues. I am delighted Naomi was bold enough to take the time she needed away from the sport and the press to figure some things out. I tell people all the time you have to do what is best for you. You have to be intentional about maintaining your self-care.

When I wrote this portion of the book it was the first week in June 2021 and I was in Mission Valley, California. Normally around this time I, along with thousands of ministers, would be in Hampton, Virginia at the Hampton University Ministers' Conference. But due to COVID-19, the university thought it best to hold a virtual conference. Since it was virtual, I decided to head out west to have my own personal retreat and finish

---

3. https://www.instagram.com/p/CPi9kJHJfxO.

this book. I did that because all of us need time away to get restored and work through our issues. Whether you are married or single, you need a place you can go and retreat and come back refreshed.

I came to California to get away from everything that gives me anxiety and triggers my depression. Thankfully I have an amazing wife who knew I needed a few days to meditate and be creative. Many people reject the importance of self-care. As for me, I have embraced it and will continue to do so, and I will not feel bad about it either. You do not have to stay in a place where people want to continue to reject who you are just to satisfy their own insecurities. Be bold, and reject their rejection of you. Be free; be secure in who you are. Be happy with who you are and what you are becoming. Life is too short to live for someone else. Live for you. Be unapologetic, be determined, just be you.

It's not too late to follow your dreams and do it for yourself, not for anyone else

When you are really serious about following your dreams, you have to take some drastic measures. For instance, I've known for a long time that I wanted to be a writer, but I'd never shared that part of my life with anyone. When you've been rejected so many times, you learn to keep some things to yourself. But for as long as I can remember I have dreamed of being a published author. I have self-published two books so far, and this is my third project. Whenever I write, I feel free. It is very cathartic for me to write; it feels like a weight has been lifted off my shoulders every time I write.

What is so interesting is that whenever I have moved on from a ministry or job, then that has been when I have been able to flow as a writer. So I had to make up my mind. Was I going to work at a job I hated? Drastic times call for drastic measures. After my contract was abruptly terminated at the church where I was the interim pastor, I decided to leave my regular job, unrelated to ministry, as well. I know it was a drastic move but it was a move I needed to make in order to follow my dreams. I am not advocating for anyone to just up and quit their job without being thoughtful about what to do next. I am encouraging people to be deliberate in following their dreams. You don't have to solicit advice from people who you know will question you to death about your decision. Trust your instincts and know when it is the right time for you to embark on the journey of your dreams.

Don't second-guess yourself about what your heart is saying. Instead, put all your energy into what you know will happen. When I quit my job, the only people who knew were my wife and therapist. They have been a source of encouragement that I so desperately needed. I'm not going to say you don't need people in your life to affirm you. I would rather say you need about two or three loving individuals who believe you can make it. And they will not stop cheering you on until what you have dreamed about becomes a reality. The reason I didn't tell anyone that I quit my job to become a writer, outside of my therapist and wife, was because I didn't want to hear them say the things I've already struggled with in my own mind. *Do you know how hard it is to become a published author? How are you going to pay your bills? How are you going to support your family? You need to get a job and stop all this daydreaming.* I was already battling with my own insecurities;

I didn't need additional doubt clouding my vision and crippling my creativity.

I made a conscious decision to follow my dreams and trust that I would eventually land on my feet. I have spent decades pleasing people and doing things that satisfied others, all the while dying inside. I have to live for me—and you, my dear human beings, you have to live for you.

We already know that not every day will be easy and the rain will come. Yet I hear Ms. Maya Angelou screaming from the heavens saying, "Every storm runs out of rain." It would behoove you, my friends, to continue to press on. Fight through your fears and, just like a tire being filled with air, fill yourself with endless possibilities. I don't know what your goals are in life. I have no clue what you have been dreaming about since you were a child. I am ignorant to what gets your creative juices flowing. But what I do know is we all have a limited time on this earth and the next minute is not even promised to us. So use the time you have left to accomplish as much as you can.

When my sister Rae passed away at the young age of thirty-seven, her words to me several months prior to her death were thought provoking: "If I knew I was going to die so young, I would have done so much more with my life." Now, it's not like she didn't accomplish a multiplicity of things, but imagine if she had more time. None of us knows the day or the hour when we will take our last breath. So, in the meantime, work on yourself, make time for your family, invest in your dreams, write down your goals, and live. Don't let people force-feed you their expectations of how your life is supposed to be. Rather, die of hunger before you settle on a meal that will give you permanent indigestion. Reject the narrow-minded thoughts that sometimes come from family and friends. Extinguish the temptation to say, "I'll do it tomorrow." Resist the unproven notion that you still have time. Wake up every day prepared to give your best and go to bed each night knowing that you did.

8

The Trauma of Racism

Why Is Being Black So Difficult?

Black people were brought as slaves to America in 1619. From the moment of their arrival, they have been met with torture; mental, physical, emotional, and spiritual abuse; economic hardship; food insecurities; premature death; and complete disrespect on all levels. My ancestors all the way up to my current comrades have dealt with injustice. Everywhere we turn we are faced with some sort of racism. Some white people will call the police on us for simply doing our jobs. We could be in uniform making deliveries and some random white person will have the audacity to ask us for identification. If we are sitting in Starbucks having a business meeting it can be considered suspicious, and now we can be arrested for "drinking coffee while Black." If we have fallen asleep because we've studied most of the night in a university study area, the police may question why we are there. When we are jogging down the street someone may throw a glass bottle at us. While we are bird-watching in the park someone may call the police and lie about us threatening them.

There have been countless encounters with police brutality; far too many have been unarmed and gunned down by police simply for being Black. If we play music in our cars while driving down the street, we could be in danger of being murdered. Wearing a hooded sweatshirt as we walk down the street with an Arizona iced tea and a bag of Skittles can cost us our lives. If we are dealing with mental illness there is no empathy; the only thing suitable for a Black person is a stun gun and prison time. Smoking or selling a dime bag of weed could get you five or more years in prison. But suddenly, weed is legal in some states because it makes the government money. What about all the young Black men and women locked up for selling weed? Are they going to be released and have their records expunged? Many believe cocaine was dropped off in minority neighborhoods and Black people who became addicted to it were considered animals and thrown into jail. Opioids went into white neighborhoods and they received rehab. That's some bullshit!

Every Black person knows someone directly or indirectly who has faced some form of racism, and the aftereffects have been detrimental. The racial trauma Black people face is unprecedented. It is unjust, inhumane, and needs to end now! How much more do we as Black people have to go through for these despicable acts to end? It feels like every day there is something new, a new video posted of Black people being harassed, spat on, hit with thrown bottles, and met with racial slurs. When is enough going to be enough?

Every day my mind is consumed with thoughts of what could happen to me, my wife, my two sons, and my only daughter. I get very upset when I see children who have had their lives cut short without ever having an opportunity to live. When white people say my two sons are handsome, I smile and say, "Thank you." But inside I wonder if they will still think they are cute when they are seventeen or eighteen. Will they think they are still cute after they start working out with me at the gym and have gained some muscle? Will they think they are cute, or will they consider them a threat because they have developed into strong, young Black men? I deal with some anxiety over my children's futures. I pray every day the Lord will keep them safe and they will never have a run-in with the police. I'm sure other Black parents have had these same thoughts and prayers concerning their children.

Kim and I are starting to have conversations with our children even before they become teenagers about what to do when confronted by the police. I wonder if white parents have to have safety-precaution conversations with their children about the police. All these things have occasionally caused me to lose sleep. But I continue to have faith that things will eventually get better. I'm not sure if it will happen in my lifetime, but I sure do hope it happens in my kids' lifetime.

I've been really fortunate

One summer evening, when I was about eighteen years old, I was heading home around 10 p.m. As I was driving through a green light, I happened to look to the left and saw a white man in a black Ford Crown Victoria. He was driving in the opposite direction and staring. Before I knew it, he made a quick U-turn and turned on police lights. I pulled over, rolled down my window, and kept both hands on the wheel as the police officer approached. When he got to my window, he looked at me and said, "How are you, Jamal?" I told him my name is not Jamal. The officer asked for my driver's license and registration card. I retrieved both from my glove compartment and handed them over. He walked away, ran my information, and came back to my car. The officer said, rudely, "You look like a Jamal." I retorted, "Not all Black people look alike, and maybe if you do your job right you can find Jamal. Now give me my shit so I can go." He handed me my information and I snatched it out of his hand and abruptly pulled off. Looking back at how I behaved (because of my own trauma), the officer could have easily held me up but he didn't. Thankfully it was just a brief encounter, but it could have escalated, and I hope my own children don't act that way when they are eighteen.

One Sunday morning when I was twenty-five, I was driving to church to meet my pastor at an early morning service. It was me and two other brothers from the church. We figured we would support the pastor then get some breakfast before the 11 a.m. service. As we were driving on the Meadowbrook State Parkway in Long Island, New York, a Nassau County police car sped by and then pulled in front of us. I signaled and moved into the middle lane from the left lane. The officer moved into the middle lane as well. I didn't know what was going on so I moved back over to the left lane. The officer followed suit. Now all three of us were wondering what this was all about. I moved over again to the right lane and continued driving. The officer pulled beside me, then pulled behind me and turned on her lights. I pulled over and let my window down. The police officer approached the car and asked for my license and registration. I reached for my information and handed it to her. Then she asked, "Why were you switching lanes, were you drinking?"

In my head I couldn't believe this was happening, I've seen it happen to others and witnessed it on television. I thought for sure I was going to lose my temper, and that would have totally compromised the situation and I know I wouldn't be writing this book. I thought to myself, *Racism and profiling are alive and well, and it is happening right before my very eyes.* At that moment I just wanted to get out of there with my life. I asked why she was harassing us, explaining that she was the one who had gotten in front of us and started slowing down and playing these games on a major parkway. I added that the only reason she had pulled us over is because we are Black. The officer could see I was getting agitated and told me I needed to calm down, which isn't what helps in a situation like that. I responded saying that she also needed to calm down and stop harassing Black people. Before I knew it two other police cars arrived, and the additional officers asked what the problem was. At that point, I was getting agitated, despite my best intentions, and I yelled from the car that the racist-ass police officer was the problem. One of the new officers came to the car and told me he wasn't talking to me. I interrupted and said, "But I'm talking to all of you bastards! Leave us alone!"

I'm not sure why I didn't get arrested or even shot for the way I behaved, despite my intentions. Thank God I am still here. After a few minutes the officer came back with my identification and told me to stay out of trouble. I cussed her out so bad I forgot I was going to church. I pulled off and continued my journey. I was so mad. I wanted to beat every one of their asses. But I couldn't. I had to suck it up and let it go. As we headed toward the church, the car was completely quiet. We had no words, just anger. I was so upset, but there was nothing I could do about it. Not many people can say they mouthed off to police officers and lived to tell the story. I don't know why I was so fortunate, but I was. If that situation would have happened now, I'm pretty sure I would have remained quiet. Why? Because I have a wife and three children to think about and I am the only one who takes care of my mother. Back then, all of my siblings were alive and I had no real responsibilities. As I think back, I am grateful God was watching over me and keeping me from danger. It is unfortunate I can't say the same for so many others.

So my hair is the problem?

On June 7, 2021, Elizabeth Logan wrote in *Glamour* that

> The Crown Act, a bill that makes hair-based discrimination illegal, just passed in Nevada, making it the twelfth state to ratify the law. The movement to combat hair-based discrimination is led by the CROWN (Creating a Respectful and Open World for Natural

Hair) Coalition. In many professional settings, Black women are especially penalized for wearing their hair in natural or specialized styles, but the Crown Act protects them from this. Hair-based discrimination is a racist prejudice that stems from a Eurocentric beauty standard, and it has no place in the workplace. Or anywhere, for that matter.[4]

I am delighted the state of Nevada took the appropriate steps to put this law in place. But give me a break! There needs to be a law to protect Black women's hair? If it's not one thing, it's another. Just when you think you have crossed one barrier, you are confronted with another. It seems to me that no matter how Black women try to advance they are met with petty roadblocks to stifle their potential. When Kimberlee was working for Company D, her last manager before she resigned, Natalie, made a comment about her braids. Let me remind you, Natalie is a Black woman from the West Indies. One morning, Kim happened to meet Natalie on the elevator. Natalie immediately noticed Kim's hair, saying, "I see you have braids . . . I don't wear braids, plus I don't think the board would approve." Thankfully, just before Kim was about to respond the elevator stopped on the floor Natalie was getting off on. At that point Kim was annoyed, so instead of taking her braids out, she decided to put her hair in different styles each day to further piss Natalie off.

Is that why Kim couldn't get a promotion in these companies? Because of her hairstyle? How tragic is it that Black

---

4. https://www.glamour.com/story/the-crown-act-passed-in-a-12th-state-nevada.

women are penalized for the most minuscule thing, their hair. Society looks past their brilliance, their education, their tenacity, their work ethic, their integrity, and focuses on their hair. I am not a woman, so I am unaware of the anguish they face just to get ahead. The demeaning roles they have to accept just to survive. Black women continue to carry a weight most other people in America would be unable to bear. Yet they prove to be strong and persistent in the face of consistent disrespect. It was Malcom X who said on May 22, 1962,

> The most disrespected person in America is the Black woman. The most unprotected person in America is the Black woman. The most neglected person in America is the Black woman. [...] Though the Black woman has been underrepresented, underestimated, and under-appreciated she continues to rise above the ashes of despair and prove that they are unstoppable.[5]

Bloodshed at Bible study

At most Black churches, Wednesday nights are set aside for Bible study or mid-week service. That is where you will receive a teaching from either the pastor or their associate ministers, or an out-of-town guest could be scheduled for a one-night-only revival. On Wednesday, June 17, 2015, a twenty-two-year-old white male by the name of Dylann Roof walked into Emanuel African Methodist Episcopal Church with the intention of slaughtering innocent Black people. He sat there in the church while the pastor Reverend Clementa Pinckney taught from the

---

5. https://speakola.com/political/malcolm-x-speech-to-black-women-1962.

Word of God. What was going through his mind as he sat among those nine parishioners who welcomed him with open arms into their church? In December 2016, there was a video released of Dylann confessing to FBI agents that he indeed killed nine parishioners. The agent asked him why he did it, and Dylann said, "I had to do it because somebody had to. Blacks are raping and killing white people on the streets every day."[6] (Sounds like he took a page out of Donald Trump's book when he said Mexicans are rapist and killers.) Dylann continued, "What I did is still minuscule to what they're doing to white people every day."[7] He sat in a church believing those nine Black people were murdering and raping white people. I'm pretty sure if Donald Trump were president in June 2015, he would have said there were "decent people on both sides".

The horror of that night will haunt those family members who have to live with the absence of their loved ones. In turn, the trauma of that night shook people of color to their core. We cannot even attend church without being in fear that we could be assassinated for attending or leading a Bible study.

When the Bible study was over, the group stood to close in prayer, and that is when Dylann opened fire with a Glock 41 .45-caliber handgun. After he completed his egregious crime, he walked out like nothing happened. That cold-hearted racist left them all to die, just because he felt all Black people were murderers and rapists.

How long must we endure these consistent attacks on Black lives? How do we forgive racist police officers for

6. https://www.cbsnews.com/news/dylann-roof-charleston-church-shooter-confession-notes-death-penalty-trial-racism/.
7. https://www.bbc.com/news/av/world-us-canada-37230916.

opening fire on Breonna Taylor while she was sleeping in her bed? How often do we need to give hugs to police officers who claim they accidentally walked into the wrong apartment and thought an intruder was in there? How many times do we have to yell out "I can't breathe" before they take their knees off our necks? How long must we tolerate a person who has served twenty-six years on the police force but doesn't know the difference between a taser and a gun? The double standard in America is not even subtle, it is blatant. If a white person is addicted to opioids they get rehab, but if a Black person is addicted to crack they get a prison sentence. A Black person suffering with mental illness is shot or left to lay on the ground naked. If a white person suffers from mental illness, they are treated with absolute care. Racism is a deep-rooted poison that has crippled this country for hundreds of years.

Some of the heightened racism came during the campaign and election of Donald Trump. The way he spewed his hatred for Asian people, Mexicans, and Blacks was absolutely revolting. His constant disrespect toward people of color was outrageous and yet he wasn't held accountable. His disdain for Black men who would challenge his politics prompted his early morning rhetoric on Twitter. Then, after losing the 2020 election, he turned on some members of his own party for refusing to believe the Big Lie. When that wasn't good enough, Trump fueled an insurrection on Capitol Hill that was filled with a level of violence on the Capitol building that hasn't been seen since before the Civil War.

James Baldwin once said in his book *Nothing Personal* that "The America of my experience has worshipped and nourished violence for as long as I have been on earth. The violence was being perpetrated mainly against black men, though—the strangers; and so it didn't count. But, if a society permits one portion of its citizenry to be menaced or destroyed, then, very soon, no one in society is safe." James Baldwin's words prove prophetic in light of what has taken place over the past few years. There is a Bible verse that supports the words of Baldwin: Galatians 5:15. It reads: "But if you bite and devour one another, watch out that you are not consumed by one another" (ESV). We are on the verge of devouring one another. America has a responsibility to handle its racism issue before the issue causes extinction. Again, as Baldwin said, "if a society permits one portion of its citizenry to be menaced or destroyed, then, very soon, no one in society is safe." The police officers Trump swore he loved were not safe, Republican senators he claimed to support were not safe, Republican congressmen and women were not safe. No one was safe the day the Capitol was attacked. If we are not careful, what the apostle Paul declared to the church at Galatia will come to pass. Be careful that you are not consumed by one another.

Asian hate vs. over four hundred years of deep-seated racism

Darlene Superville wrote an article for the Associated Press on May 20, 2021, about how President Joe Biden

> signed legislation to curtail a dramatic rise in hate crimes against Asian Americans and Pacific Islanders and expressed pride that lawmakers who seem to agree on little else came together against hate and racism.

Biden lavished praise on Democrats and Republicans for approving the bill by lopsided margins and sending it to the White House for his signature. Several dozen lawmakers attended the bill signing ceremony, one of the largest groups to visit the Biden White House during the pandemic.

The House approved the bill 364-62, following the Senate's 94-1 vote in April. Biden, who stressed his wish to help unite the country as he campaigned for office, said during the East Room event that fighting hate and racism should bring people together. "I'm proud today of the United States," he said.[8]

Isn't that interesting? President Biden signed a bill after four months in office to protect Asian Americans, but with some exceptions there have been few federal level bills to protect Black Americans from constant attacks. There have been constant assaults on voting rights in minority areas, or against talking about race in schools. And while police brutality may technically be illegal, it still happens more frequently than anyone realizes and especially to Black Americans. There are no discussions around reparations for descendants of slaves. But we are supposed to be content with Juneteenth being a federal holiday? What a slap in the face to the people who put Biden in office. What a gut punch to the people who always get the shitty end of the deal. When will Black lives really matter? When will we receive what we're due? When will it be our turn? Don't ask me why I am angry. Ask me what triggers my

---

8. https://apnews.com/article/crime-hate-crimes-bills-health-coronavirus-pandemic-98c62be02eb2537d78ca7a4c36530a18.

anger. My frustration is real, my anger is legitimate, and my pain hurts like hell. I don't know when our punishment for being born Black will end. I don't know when Black people will receive their due. What I do know is that we are tired and have had enough of the lies, letdowns, and betrayals. It is time for America to pay up. No more empty promises and no more bounced checks. We deserve better. Black lives matter!

9
It's Time to Reinvent Yourself

re·in·vent/ˌrēinˈvent/Change (something) so much that it appears to be entirely new

I am not the same person that I was last year or five, ten, or fifteen years ago. I am in a different place mentally, physically, and spiritually. The things that would push me to a place of uncontrollable rage have lost their hold on me. What would keep me up at night then has no room in my mental Rolodex now. The pain of yesterday and the anxiety that tried to force itself on me cannot invade my spirit. I have learned to control my emotions and not give unqualified people access to my life. Practicing meditation and being persistent in my devotion to God has helped transform my way of thinking. My daily discipline of prayer, exercise, and healthy eating continues to help me grow in ways I never could have imagined.

I am genuinely happy with my life and the wonderful things on the horizon. I surely do not profess to know all the answers to life. But I am confident that when you exercise faith in God and in yourself there is no telling how far you can go and all you will accomplish. Reinventing myself is not a New Year's resolution that will cease to exist by mid-March. It is a calculated process I take seriously each day. When I wake up in the morning, I am purposeful about how my day will be. I decline any interruption that will disturb my peace and compromise my integrity. I seek to ensure my relationships with others are healthy and that we complement each other rather than being in competition with each other. I strive to inspire my children to be better than me and never settle for the ordinary but strive for the exceptional. The bond I have with my wife is reflective of our unconditional love and ability to always remember how fortunate we are to have one another in our lives.

Reinventing myself comes with relinquishing the grip I have on my regrets and taking advantage of the wonderful opportunities I have had. This transformation didn't happen overnight. It took time. I had to really examine where my life was going and ask myself whether I was pleased with the direction. This happened after my contract was abruptly terminated at Hartford Baptist. I knew then I couldn't keep going backward and trying to fit into places that weren't interested in a good work ethic or my philosophy as a man and a minister. Those things are important to me, and I made a conscious decision to never, ever compromise them again. I have stuck with that plan of action, and I am pleased with its outcome.

Many of us find ourselves asking whether there is more for us to do that would glorify God, perhaps especially by serving those faced with undeviating misfortune. I don't just want to have financial freedom, I want to see others make decisions that will break the chains of hopelessness. I want to see people come in direct contact with their purpose in life. There are so many people who have gone through life without ever having a connection with their purpose, calling, and what drives and motivates them—what causes their creativity to expand in areas where they thought they wouldn't be accepted. They instead have been cemented into life's pre-written script, not knowing they have a shot to rewrite the story. You don't have to accept what is thrown at you; it is not mandatory to tolerate what is intolerable. Knowing your worth is a superpower few people exercise. When you know who you are, where you are going, and what you are worth, you cannot be bamboozled into anything less than what you are destined to be.

I had a hard time finding myself and finding my rhythm. When that was obvious, people tried to mold me into what they thought I should be. When I was the most vulnerable, the most insecure I've ever been, it attracted users, manipulators, miscreants, liars, and leeches. They were the epitome of wolves in sheep's clothing. Their words of deceit trapped me for some time into believing I couldn't make it without them. It forced me into a dark place. I thought for sure there was no way out. I knew I would die trying to prove I was worthy. Those were some bleak and miserable times. When I cried, I was considered weak. When I held back tears, I was deemed arrogant and heartless.

I didn't know what to do and I lost myself trying to please people who never truly cared about my development as a man or a minister. I was used only for my gift of hyping the crowd, and the moment I tried to step out of that box I was blackballed. So, when I say you must be confident in who you are and what you are destined to be, it doesn't come from a place of textbook teaching. It comes from a place of real-life trauma that tried to consume me, but I never realized I was wearing bunker gear. I may have felt the heat but it never had the chance to burn my drive to be better.

My drive comes from witnessing other people who have tried and failed in their lives, yet they keep getting back up and going after what they want, regardless of their current circumstances. And after some time, they have either reached or exceeded their goals. I admire people like Steve Jobs, Barack Obama, T. D. Jakes, Noel Jones, Jamal Bryant, Steve Harvey, Oprah Winfrey, and Tyler Perry. These are people who have faced an enormous number of challenges; some of them have been homeless, broke, abused, humiliated, overlooked; however, today they are household names. They didn't give up, and they pursued their call with relentless energy. I took what these brilliant individuals have done and created my own mantra, which is "You can do it, no matter what." I stand by that phrase, and I exercise it every day.

Reinventing myself has meant relentlessly pursuing the things I know I can have. I think many of us tend to doubt other people's ability to achieve their dreams. Fortunately, some of us realize that tendency and do the work of ignoring people's opinions to let go of those doubts. Once we have reprogrammed ourselves, we realize our role is not to put out the light from anyone's dreams but to fuel other people's fires. I have met people who made it their business to tell me what I couldn't do. As with anything, refutation or affirmation, when you hear it enough you will eventually believe it. I had to battle with people who made it their personal mission to hinder my progress and determination. There have been times I barely had anyone I could trust and those I thought I could trust had hidden motives. Eventually I started to believe their lies, and that caused a snowball effect. For a long time, I was frozen and afraid to try anything new. Whenever I tried something different all I heard was, "What do you want to do that for?" or "You should leave that to people who have a chance." Those traumatic experiences are crippling and if you are not careful, they can wipe you out before you have the chance to get started.

So, what did I do? I silently moved away and began to tell myself, *I can have whatever I put my mind to.* I was strategic. I would privately work on things I knew people would think I couldn't do, and when they were all complete, I would make my debut. I talked about moving in silence in the rejection chapter and how it bodes well to operate discreetly until the opportune time comes to release your idea. I put that into practice, and I continue to follow that same approach. I was able to escape my naysayers before they had the opportunity to crush my confidence. Now, you will always have people who will doubt your ability to get things done; the secret is to not allow that energy into your space. Be indefatigable in your pursuit of greatness. Tune out everyone who dares to say you can't, and let your work speak louder than their doubts about who you are.

One day I saw an Instagram post that said: "I just want to remind you that some of the best days of your life haven't even happened yet." Those are some life-changing, get-up-out-of-your-stupor type of words. Hearing those words at twenty-five is probably not as effective as hearing them at forty-three or fifty-three. But hearing them when you have made it through so much pain is very refreshing. Imagine for a moment you thought it was all over, but in all actuality, you were just in your trial stage and now it's time for you to fly.

This is your moment to be great. This is your chance to experience life on your terms with God's breath blowing in your direction. You've survived what has destroyed others. You are the poster child for "I don't look like what I've been through." And to add to that, your best days haven't come to fruition yet. You are on track to becoming everything you have dreamed of. You are on target to accomplish things you thought were out of reach. Now that you know there is so much more that hasn't happened, you have to protect your sanity. Disqualify those who will attempt to undercut what you have worked so hard to get. Fight for your future. You deserve better.

Reinventing myself shows me who is not allowed to come with me into this next season of my life. I remember a few years ago I invited a friend to a work event where we were raising money for an HIV/AIDS organization. All the executives were there, along with the CEO and chairman of the board. It was a big deal. While everyone was introducing their families and friends to the staff, I introduced my friend Jeff to my manager, Mike. Mike extended his hand to greet Jeff and the most embarrassing thing happened. Jeff looked at him, rolled his eyes, waved him off, and walked off. If the earth could have opened at that very moment, I would have jumped in and allowed it to swallow me whole. I apologized profusely to Mike. Mike looked at me with a great big smile and said, "You cannot invite everyone to the next level. They will either embarrass you or cause you to lose out. You have a decision to make." Then he walked away. I knew then that if I wanted to be successful, if I wanted to do extraordinary things, there were some people who couldn't come along.

When the work event was over, I asked Jeff what his problem was and explained that was my boss who he had blown off. I knew what Jeff's problem was: he was jealous; I just wanted him to admit it and apologize for embarrassing me. Jeff said, "So?" I was shocked and relieved at the same time—shocked he would do something like that and relieved I finally had the courage to do something that needed to be done. I cut him off in that moment. I am still cordial when I see him, but he knows our friendship is not the same.

When you know you are on your way somewhere you have to make the hard choices; you have to do what is right for you and refuse to allow anyone to hinder your growth. The problem is people are used to the old you. They don't know how to handle the new and improved you. They can't understand how it is that you both come from the same environment but you have excelled while they are still stuck. You are not responsible for their lack of preparation; you are not responsible for their lack of integrity and work ethic. You have worked hard to get where you are and they have to realize you are not willing to sacrifice your present or your future because they take issue with who you have become. Don't get me wrong; it is difficult to distance yourself from people you have considered family. But when you recognize all of the opportunities you will miss out on because of their disregard for your future, you will eventually come around—hopefully sooner than later. Many people started with me on this journey, but as life would have it, we all took different paths—some for the best and some for the worst. I, like others, chose to be better, and I will not apologize for bettering myself. No more making excuses for people who refuse to change.

Reinventing myself means that I can no longer stand in fear of what I may lose. When we are in the process of reinventing ourselves, we are often afraid people will leave us during our transformation. So we tone down our language of acceleration to appease stagnation. Someone once said, "Don't be afraid of losing people. Be afraid of losing yourself trying to please everyone." The time is now for you to stop trying to please people. This is important because whenever you are consumed with trying to make others happy, you lose the value of who you are. When you lose yourself, those same people will refuse to help you find yourself. You will be left discouraged, disappointed, angry, and full of regret.

I want you to come to terms with who you are and sever the ties that bind. I can tell you from personal experience it is not worth sacrificing yourself and your ambitions for someone else's agenda. Work on yourself continuously, know what a good fit for you is, and know when to say no. You will be better off in the long run. You have so much to live for. Start living for yourself today.

The old you has no place in your new environment

There is a scripture verse that continues to hold true in my heart. Matthew 9:16–17 (ESV):

> No one puts a piece of unshrunk cloth on an old garment, for the patch tears away from the garment, and a worse tear is made. Neither is new wine put into old wineskins. If it is, the skins burst and the wine is spilled and the skins are destroyed. But new wine is put into fresh wineskins, and so both are preserved.

I love this scripture because it pulls no punches. It clearly tells you that you cannot cover up the old with a new environment and you cannot take what is new and mix it with the old because both will be destroyed. Basically, you have to change in order to get better results. We spend a lot of time unpacking other people and their issues, but we don't spend nearly enough time unpacking ours.

I've shared in this book that I have a nasty temper, and when I have lost my temper there is no going back. I had to realize that if I was going to do something worthwhile in this life, I had to get myself together. I could no longer make excuses for my ridiculous and childlike behavior. Something had to give. I had to get control of my temper or it would eventually cost me. When I realized I missed out on so many ventures I had to stop blaming haters and the environment. The issue was me. The person holding me back from destiny was me. The moment I realized that fact I started working on myself. I prayed harder and worked out more consistently. I had to discipline myself if anyone was going to take me seriously.

There is a Proverb that says, "A man without self-control is like a city broken into and left without walls" (25:28 ESV). If you cannot control yourself, that means anyone can push your buttons and you will explode. That was my issue. Too many people were able to push my buttons, and after I exploded, they walked away laughing and I was left to pick up the pieces. The time came when I had to put a stop to my unpredictable behavior. It was getting too messy and I was about to crash. I didn't want that life anymore and I didn't want my children to see me act in such an awful way. I did it for them and I did it for me. The moment I took control of my emotions is the moment I changed. I'd wasted enough time going in the way of destruction and confusion; it was time to move in the way of progress.

There is a new environment waiting for us; it is waiting because we have the gifts and talents to make it better. We hold the key to our change; let's not throw it away because we cannot control our emotions. Protect your peace at all costs. Guard your integrity, because once you lose it, it will be an excruciating task to get it back.

I get a do-over

I am preparing to move my family to California. We have been praying about this move and doing the research for a long time. We decided that 2021 would be the year we finally pulled the trigger and said "Goodbye east and hello west." Kim and I believe California is the place for us to do our do-over.

Not many people can start over fresh; they are too busy living in their past. I've been there and done that for far too long. Nothing good comes from living in something you know you cannot change. I cannot change the mistakes I have made in relationships, places of employment, and churches. Yes, I have made my fair share of mistakes. There are some things I wish I could have handled better, but at least I know what to do if those types of situations present themselves again. I've learned how to let stuff go for my mental and physical health. I'm at peace with relationships that will never be reconciled. I have found strength in moving forward in life, even if that means there is distance from those who tried to hold me back.

I know I will probably make more mistakes in California because I am human. But I can assure you there will be no temper tantrum from me. There will be no out-of-control reaction to a situation that is clearly in God's hands. What you will see is someone who is grateful God gave him another chance to get things right. I am so proud of where I have come. I am grateful for all of the lessons I have learned along the way. I am thankful for the people who have hurt me because I know the difference between the counterfeit and authentic. I am delighted to know the people I have hurt have forgiven me. Whether they forgave me or not, I was genuinely sorry for the pain I caused.

I think when the opportunity for you to start over comes your way you should be thrilled. I am ecstatic God didn't forget about me. There were days I thought, *This must be it; there is nothing left for me to do.* Then I would hear a faint whisper saying, *I am not through with you yet, so live.* Wherever you are in life, I want to tell you God is not through with you yet, so live. Live until all your mistakes become a memory. Live until all the stones thrown at you become stepping-stones into your future. Live like you know tomorrow is not promised. Live so your children can see that no matter how low you go there is always a chance to bounce back. Live until all your dreams come true. Live like God owes you nothing but you owe him everything. Live, because trauma can fade if you keep trying to overcome and it will not always have its hold on you. Regardless of the trauma I am certain you can achieve your goals. Live a life that is fulfilling, enjoy happiness and love with another human being, and enjoy endless possibilities.

You will get through this. Help is there when you are ready.

Acknowledgments

I never thought the words, "I am a writer," would ever leave my mouth. I've always been intrigued by how writers come up with concepts and storylines. It amazes me how dedicated they are to their craft and that has truly inspired me to write.

I must begin with overwhelming gratitude for my wife, Kimberlee, and my three children, Brendan, Sasha, and Noah, for always giving me time and space to write. I love you with my entire being! Special thanks to my mother who always said, "Boy, turn off that television and read a book." Love you, Mom!

I want to thank OurPrayer, a service of Guideposts that really opened my eyes to different genres of books and writers. I am grateful for Dr. Pablo Diaz and Dr. Peola Hicks for showing me a whole new world outside of the four walls of the church. I am thankful for my Connecticut Prayer line that encouraged me to keep writing. Special thanks to every pastor and preacher that has provoked me to dig deeper in everything I do.

Thank you to Dr. David Morris who has taken a chance on me and continues to push me in my writing. Thank you to Sia Henry who initiated the first edits to this project. You are amazing.

To every author that continues to share their story, I am inspired by your dedication.

Lastly, to everyone that has experienced and survived trauma, I've written this book for us as a testimony that we are unstoppable.

About the Author

Lemuel R. T. Blackett is a writer and ordained local church pastor who has served in ministry for more than twenty years, including as an associate of partnership development at Guideposts' *OurPrayer*. Originally from London, Blackett grew up in Roosevelt, New York. He is a graduate of Eastern Baptist School of Religion and is pursuing an MDiv at Knox Theological Seminary. Currently he lives in San Diego, California with his wife, Kimberlee, and their three children, Brendan, Sasha, and Noah. Learn more at lemuelblackett.org.